Latin American Samba

THE IMPERIAL SOCIETY OF TEACHERS OF DANCING
IMPERIAL HOUSE, 22/26 PAUL STREET
LONDON EC2A 4QE
TELEPHONE NO: 020 7377 1577   FAX NO: 020 7247 8979

e-mail:sales@istd.org
website:http://www.istd.org

Issued by the

Latin American Dance Faculty Committee

Original published in separate parts between
July 1971 and July 1973

First Edition (5000 copies) July 1974

Second Edition revised and enlarged (4000 copies) 1975

Third Edition revised and enlarged (5000 copies) 1978

Fourth Edition revised and enlarged (3000 copies) 1981

Fifth Edition enlarged (2000 copies) 1983

Sixth Edition revised Part 4 Samba (2000 copies) 2000

Sixth Edition revised Part 4 Samba reprinted with amendments 2002

FIGURES

(Fellowship figures continued overleaf)

FIGURES (continued)

Fellow

FOREWORD

The book you are about to read was compiled by the Latin American Dance Faculty of the Imperial Society of Teachers of Dancing, their experience covering every facet of teaching from the beginner and medallist to the competitor and professional examination candidate. This is a book for teachers by teachers, and is a reference book to enable teachers to develop the rhythm and character of the dances in their pupils at all levels.

A close study of our leading Latin exponents, past and present, was carried out and every modern development considered.

Figures have been added to the syllabus according to popularity, and the existing technique has been clarified, resulting in an easy to read analysis in chart form.

It will be noted from the Latin American syllabus that the figures for the professional candidate have been carefully graded to be consistent with those of the medallist. For example, in the theoretical section the Student - Teacher is required to have knowledge of the figures best suited to beginners, social dancing and the Social Dance Tests. The Associate syllabus embraces the Bronze medal figures, Licentiate the Silver, and Fellow the Gold. However, in the practical demonstration section of the professional examinations candidates may include figures from the next level if they wish, although no technical questions will be asked on these figures. For example, the Student - Teacher may dance figures from the Associate syllabus while the Associate may use figures from the Licentiate and the Licentiate from the Fellowship syllabus.

Teachers are reminded to read the interesting alternatives for some of the figures listed at a lower level; knowledge of these developments will be required for the higher examinations.

This is the official Latin American Technique book upon which the Imperial Society examinations are based. Please refer to the syllabus for further requirements.

Note for teachers who are coaching couples for Juvenile or Novice competitions held under BDC rules. Please refer to the Rule Book published by the British Dance Council for the list of figures and holds allowed for these grades

ABBREVIATIONS USED IN THIS BOOK

L	Left
R	Right
LF	Left Foot
RF	Right Foot
LOD	Line of Dance
DW	Diagonally to wall
DC	Diagonally to centre
B	Ball of foot
H	Heel
T	Toe
F	Flat
BF	Ball flat
HF	Heel flat
WF	Whole foot
IE	Inside edge
PR	Pressure
Fwd	Forward
Bwd	Backward
Diag	Diagonally
CBMP	Contra Body Movement Position
OP	Outside Partner
PP	Promenade Position
CPP	Counter Promenade Position
LSP	Left Side Position
RSP	Right Side Position
St	Student - Teacher
A	Associate
L	Licentiate
F	Fellowship

Professional Candidates   Please note it is better not to use abbreviations verbally

4

PLEASE READ THESE PAGES BEFORE PROGRESSING TO CHARTS

TIME SIGNATURE	2/4 (2 beats to a bar of music)
ACCENT	There is a musical accent on the first beat of each bar with a percussive accent on the second beat
TEMPO	50 bars per minute (The speed at which the music is played)
	The tempo given is as required by the British Dance Council for Championships. Slight deviations are acceptable for examinations and tests

RHYTHM

The Samba is a dance of contrasting rhythms. Within the syllabus the following rhythms are used

Count	Beat value	Alternative method of counting
1. 2	1. 1	S S
1 a 2	3/4. 1/4. 1	S a S
1 a 2 a 1 a 2	3/4. 1/4. 3/4. 1/4. 3/4. 1/4. 1	S a S a S a S
1. 2. 3	3/4. 1/2. 3/4	(No alternative)
SQQ	1. 1/2. 1/2	1. 2 and
SQQQQQQ	1. 1/2. 1/2. 1/2. 1/2. 1/2. 1/2	1. 2 and 1 and 2 and
QQS	1/2. 1/2. 1	1 and 2
SSQQS	1. 1. 1/2. 1/2. 1	1. 2. 1 and 2

In the charts the numerical rhythmic count is given on figures where the normal Samba bounce action is used, and on the "1.2.3" timing. "Slows" and "Quicks" are given on all other figures. In the examination room candidates may use the method of their choice

PHRASING

Most Samba music is written in two bar phrases. It is desirable, and more pleasurable, for each figure or group of movements to commence at the beginning of a musical phrase. This is achieved by choosing the correct Precede or Follow to suit the phrasing

NORMAL HOLD AND POISE

Stand with feet apart, facing partner about 15 cms (6 inches) apart, with the head erect, the body naturally upright and the shoulders down

The Man's right hand is placed on the Lady's left shoulder blade and the Lady's left arm rests lightly on his right arm following the curve of his arm to the shoulder. The Man's left hand is raised in a gentle curve to the level of the eyes. The Lady's right hand is placed in the Man's left hand with her fingers between his thumb and first finger. The hands are lightly clasped

BODY POSITIONS AND HOLDS USED IN SAMBA

These refer to the Lady's position in relation to the Man and should be stated prior to giving Foot Positions or a description. Where necessary, for clarity, reference is made to a Body Position in the Foot Position column

1   **CLOSED POSITION (St,A,L&F)**

      Facing partner, slightly apart, normal hold or left to right hand hold

2   **CONTACT POSITION (F)**

      Facing partner with light body contact and normal hold

3 PROMENADE POSITION (St,A,L&F)

Lady on Man's right side with the Man's right and Lady's left side towards each other, slightly apart, and the opposite side of the body turned outwards to form the shape of a "V". Normal hold

4 OPEN PROMENADE POSITION (St,A,L&F)

As Promenade Position with left hand holding Lady's right hand. The distance apart may vary considerably and become more open, depending on the figure danced
(F) Right hand on Lady's back, left to right hand hold released

5 COUNTER PROMENADE POSITION (A,L&F)

Lady on Man's left side with Man's left side and Lady's right side towards each other, slightly apart, and the opposite side of the body turned outwards to form the shape of a "V". Normal hold

6 OPEN COUNTER PROMENADE POSITION (St,A,L&F)

As Counter Promenade Position, slightly more apart. The distance apart may vary considerably and become more open, depending on the figure danced

Holds

1 Left hand holding Lady's right hand
2 Left hand on Lady's back **(F)**

7   RIGHT SIDE POSITION (L&F)

Lady on Man's right side, both facing the same way. Hold as required for figure used

8   RIGHT SHADOW POSITION (A,L&F)

Lady on Man's right side, slightly in advance, both facing the same way. Right hand placed on or just below Lady's right shoulder blade, left hand holding Lady's left hand, wrist or lower arm (or no hold)

9   RIGHT CONTRA POSITION (F)

Man and Lady moving, or positioned to move, towards partner's right side

10   LEFT CONTRA POSITION (F)

Man and Lady moving, or positioned to move, towards partner's left side

FOOT POSITIONS

These refer to the position of one foot in relation to the other when the foot has arrived in position; for example, forward, back, side, etc. Promenade Position, Counter Promenade Position, Open Counter Promenade Position, CBMP, etc are also given in the Foot Position column for clarity

It must be understood that when moving the foot from one Open Position to another the leg must always track "under" the body

CONTRA BODY MOVEMENT POSITION (CBMP) (ST,A,L&F)

A forward or backward step placed in line with, or slightly across the line of the other foot

CUBAN CROSS (St,A,L&F)

This term denotes a position where, for example, the RF is behind LF, right toe opposite or just past left heel, toe turned out. (Example Man's step 2 of Whisk to Left). The exact distance between the toe of the back foot and heel of the front foot will depend on the dancer's own physique or the figure danced. This also applies when the LF is behind RF in the same position, and when the RF or LF is in front, heel opposite or just past the toe, with toe turned out

REPLACE (St, A,L&F)

This denotes a step where foot pressure is momentarily released from the floor before placing the step on the same spot (Example Step 3 of Whisk)

PART WEIGHT

A step where the weight is centralised between the two feet

MINIMAL WEIGHT

Less than half weight is taken on to the foot

ALIGNMENT

Because the Samba is a progressive dance alignments are given, and are required in the examination room

Alignment in this dance refers to the position of the foot in relation to the room

On forward, steps and some side steps and closing steps, the term "facing" is used. For example, "facing LOD", "facing diagonally to centre", etc

On backward, steps and some side steps and closing steps, the term "backing" is used. For example, "backing wall", "backing diagonally to centre", etc

Direction is given where the toe is turned out on a forward or backward step. For example "against LOD"

The term "pointing" is used on a step where the body has made less or more turn than the foot

On a step in Promenade or Counter Promenade Position the direction of the step and the alignment of the foot will often differ, therefore both are given. For example "Moving along Line of Dance, facing diagonally to wall"

ALIGNMENT IN RELATION TO ROOM

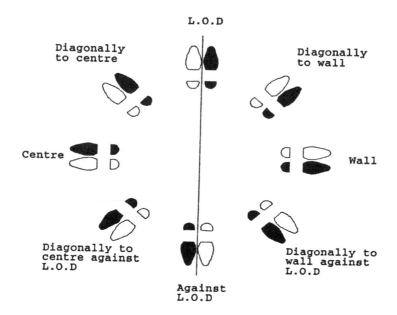

AMOUNT OF TURN

This is measured from the alignment of one step to the alignment of the following step

AMOUNTS OF TURN
(This diagram represents one complete turn)

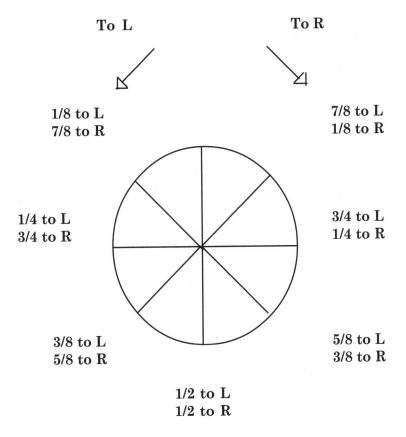

To L

To R

1/8 to L
7/8 to R

7/8 to L
1/8 to R

1/4 to L
3/4 to R

3/4 to L
1/4 to R

3/8 to L
5/8 to R

5/8 to L
3/8 to R

1/2 to L
1/2 to R

FOOTWORK

This refers briefly to the parts of the foot used when taking a step. For example "ball flat", "ball", "toe", "heel flat" etc

Points to Remember

1   Forward steps are normally "ball, flat". Exceptions; "heel, flat" on Man's first step of Corta Jaca and Natural Roll, and Lady's fourth step of Natural Roll
Lady's steps of Plait are danced on ball of foot although heel may lightly touch the floor

2   The heel does not lower on steps taking a 1/4 beat of music (Footwork is "ball", "toe" or "inside edge of toe" depending on figure danced)

3   Steps taking a 1/2 beat of music are "ball", "ball flat" or "toe" depending on figure danced

LEADS

Leads may be loosely divided into four categories as follows

1	**Weight changes**	Lady will follow Man's change of weight
2	**Physical**	Man conveys the lead by increasing the tone in his arm(s) resulting in pressure felt through the hands. Lady responds with matching tone and will continue to move in the direction indicated, until the Man's hand restricts her movement
3	**Shaping**	Man conveys the position required by "shaping" his body and arms. Weight changes are assumed
4	**Visual**	When dancing without hold Lady may copy the Man's steps

The Leads are given in the charts as a guide but have not been explained in great detail thus allowing for individual interpretation

PRECEDES AND FOLLOWS

The listed Precedes and Follows given for each figure are all that are necessary for the theoretical section of the professional examination; these are clearly classified for Student - Teacher, Associate, Licentiate and Fellow

The Student - Teacher will be required to know one Precede and Follow to each figure, the Associate two, and the Licentiate and Fellow three (where applicable)

SAMBA BOUNCE (ST,A,L,&F)

The normal bounce action which is so characteristic of the Samba can briefly be described as a slight flexing of the knees on the first 1/2 of the beat and a slight straightening on the second 1/2 of the beat

There are two beats to a bar in Samba music and two complete bounce actions to the bar

Normal bounce is created by the use of the knee, ankle and instep of the leg supporting most of the weight, the other knee working in sympathy. It is even, smooth and subtle and never exaggerated

Bounce is not used where there is a "Quick" in the timing of the figure EXCEPTION:- Cruzados Walk and Locks

Bounce action is used on all figures having the count of " 1 a 2" (3 steps to a bar)

(Detailed description overleaf)

SAMBA BOUNCE (continued)

Example of Bounce action on 1 - 3 of the Natural Basic Movement

Commence with feet together and knees slightly flexed.

This action is commenced during the second half of the preceding beat.

1 Commence to slightly straighten the knees and with pressure through ball of LF, move RF fwd with slight pressure on ball of foot

2 Continuing to slightly straighten the knees place RF fwd on ball of foot

3 Take weight onto RF, slightly flexing the knees & lowering the heel (the knees will continue to flex slightly after the heel has lowered)

4 Commencing to slightly straighten the knees, draw LF towards RF
Without weight but with pressure on ball of foot

5 Close LF to RF without weight but with pressure

6 Continuing to slightly straighten the knees take minimal weight to LF, replace weight to RF on ball of foot, slightly flexing the knees & lowering the heel. (the knees will continue to flex slightly after the heel has lowered)

Constant rules

The bounce action explained above is used on all figures having the count of "1 a 2" although the foot positions may differ, as may the footwork of the second step

All steps danced on "a" counts are without weight, taking minimal weight on to foot as the next step is placed

EXCEPTION:- An exception is the Travelling, Circular and Spot Volta.

Part weight is taken as step 3 is placed.

NOTES

1   BASIC MOVEMENTS

NATURAL BASIC MOVEMENT (ST,A,L&F)

Commence in Closed Position. Use Bounce action

MAN	Foot Position	Alignment	Amount of Turn	Foot-work	Lead	Count
1	RF fwd	According to previous figure	No turn, or up to 1/4 to R over 1-6	BF	Weight change	1
2	Close LF to RF without weight			B (Press-ure)	Retain tone in arms	a
3	Take minimal weight to LF and replace weight to RF			BF	Weight change	2
4	LF back			BF	"	1
5	Close RF to LF without weight			B (Press-ure)	Retain tone in arms	a
6	Take minimal weight to RF and replace weight to LF			BF	Weight change	2

May be repeated

Note	If preferred the Natural Basic Movement may be danced using four steps as follows	
1	RF fwd (BF)	1
2	Close LF to RF with pressure but without weight (BF)	2
3	LF back (BF)	1
4	Close RF to LF with pressure but without weight (BF)	2

The Bounce action is minimal

NATURAL BASIC MOVEMENT (continued)

LADY	Foot Position	Alignment	Amount of Turn	Footwork	Count
1	LF back	According to previous figure	No turn, or up to 1/4 to R over 1-6	BF	1
2	Close RF to LF without weight			B (Pressure)	a
3	Take minimal weight to RF and replace weight to LF			BF	2
4	RF fwd			BF	1
5	Close LF to RF without weight			B (Pressure)	a
6	Take minimal weight to LF and replace weight to RF			BF	2

May be repeated

Note   If preferred the Natural Basic Movement may be danced using four steps as follows

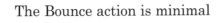

1	LF back (BF)	1
2	Close RF to LF with pressure but without weight (BF)	2
3	RF fwd (BF)	1
4	Close LF to RF with pressure but without weight (BF)	2

The Bounce action is minimal

NATURAL BASIC MOVEMENT (continued)

Precedes (St,A,L&F)   Any syllabus figure ended facing partner with weight on LF

Precedes to 4 - 6
(St)	Whisk to R
(A)	Corta Jaca
(L)	RF Back Rock
(F)	Plait (ended on RF)

Follows   (St,A,L&F)   Any syllabus figure commenced with RF when facing partner, depending on alignment

1-3 of Natural Basic Movement may precede any syllabus figure to be commenced with LF, when facing partner, depending on alignment

Note   (St,A,L&F)

When used as a Precede to Travelling Bota Fogos Fwd, commence the Natural Basic Movement facing LOD and turn 1/8 L over 2 and 3. 4-6 are then danced with Lady outside

When used as a Follow to Travelling Bota Fogos Fwd the first step is outside partner. Turn 1/8 R over 2 and 3 to face partner

REVERSE BASIC MOVEMENT (ST,A,L&F)

Commence in Closed Position. Use Bounce action

MAN	Foot Position	Alignment	Amount of Turn	Foot-work	Lead	Count
1	LF fwd	According to previous figure	No turn, or up to 1/4 to L over 1-6	BF	Weight change	1
2	Close RF to LF without weight			B (Press-ure)	Retain tone in arms	a
3	Take minimal weight to RF and replace weight to LF			BF	Weight change	2
4	RF back			BF	"	1
5	Close LF to RF without weight			B (Press-ure)	Retain tone in arms	a
6	Take minimal weight to LF and replace weight to RF			BF	Weight change	2

May be repeated

Note   If preferred the Reverse Basic Movement may be danced
using four steps as follows
1   LF fwd (BF)   1
2   Close RF to LF with pressure but without weight (BF)   2
3   RF back (BF)   1
4   Close LF to RF with pressure but without weight (BF)   2

The Bounce action is minimal

REVERSE BASIC MOVEMENT (continued)

LADY	Foot Position	Alignment	Amount of Turn	Footwork	Count
1	RF back	According to previous figure	No turn, or up to 1/4 to L over 1-6	BF	1
2	Close LF to RF without weight			B (Pressure)	a
3	Take minimal weight to LF and replace weight to RF			BF	2
4	LF fwd			BF	1
5	Close RF to LF without weight			B (Pressure)	a
6	Take minimal weight to RF and replace weight to LF			BF	2

May be repeated

Note If preferred the Reverse Basic Movement may be danced using four steps as follows

1	RF back (BF)	1
2	Close LF to RF with pressure but without weight (BF)	2
3	LF Fwd (BF)	1
4	Close RF to LF with pressure but without weight (BF)	2

The Bounce action is minimal

REVERSE BASIC MOVEMENT (continued)

Precedes	**(St)**	Any syllabus figure ended facing partner with weight on RF

Precedes to 4 - 6

	(St)	Whisk to L
	(L)	LF Back Rock
	(F)	Plait (ended on LF)

Follows	**(St)**	Any syllabus figure commenced with LF when facing partner, depending on alignment

1-3 of Reverse Basic Movement may precede any syllabus figure to be commenced with RF, when facing partner, depending on alignment

SIDE BASIC MOVEMENT

This figure may be danced in place of the Natural or Reverse Basic Movements taking the first step to side. All other technical details are the same

(This is a useful introductory figure for beginners and for Social Dance and Pre - Bronze Tests)

PROGRESSIVE BASIC MOVEMENT (ST,A,L&F)

Commence in Closed Position. Use Bounce action

MAN	Foot Position	Alignment	Amount of Turn	Foot-work	Lead	Count
1	RF fwd	Facing DW	No turn	BF	Weight change	1
2	Close LF to RF without weight	"	"	B (Press-ure)	Retain tone in arms	a
3	Take minimal weight to LF and replace weight to RF	"	"	BF	Weight change	2
4	LF to side	"	"	BF	"	1
5	Close RF to LF without weight	"	"	B (Press-ure)	Retain tone in arms	a
6	Take minimal weight to RF and replace weight to LF	"	"	BF	Weight change	2

May be repeated

Note   If preferred the Progressive Basic Movement may be danced using four steps as follows

1	RF fwd (BF)	1
2	Close LF to RF with pressure but without weight (BF)	2
3	LF to side (BF)	1
4	Close RF to LF with pressure but without weight (BF)	2

The Bounce action is minimal

LADY	Foot Position	Alignment	Amount of Turn	Footwork	Count
1	LF back	Backing DW	No turn	BF	1
2	Close RF to LF without weight	"	"	B (Pressure)	a
3	Take minimal weight to RF and replace weight to LF	"	"	BF	2
4	RF to side	"	"	BF	1
5	Close LF to RF without weight	"	"	B (Pressure)	a
6	Take minimal weight to LF and replace weight to RF	"	"	BF	2

May be repeated

Note   If preferred the Progressive Basic Movement may be danced using four steps as follows

1   LF back (BF)   1

2   Close RF to LF with pressure but without weight (BF)   2

3   RF to side (BF)   1

4   Close LF to RF with pressure but without weight (BF)   2

The Bounce action is minimal

PROGRESSIVE BASIC MOVEMENT (continued)

Precedes (St,A,L&F) Any syllabus figure ended facing partner
with weight on LF, facing DW

Follows **(St)** Natural Basic Movement - Progressive
Basic Movement

(A&L) Corta Jaca

(F) Natural Roll

NOTES

2 WHISKS

WHISK TO LEFT (ST,A,L&F)

Commence in Closed Position. Use Bounce action

MAN	Foot Position	Alignment	Amount of Turn	Foot-work	Lead	Count
1	LF to side	Facing wall	No turn	BF	Weight change	1
2	RF behind LF without weight (Cuban Cross)	"	"	T (Press-ure)	Retain tone in arms	a
3	Take minimal weight to RF and replace weight to LF	"	"	BF	Weight change	2

Other alignments may be used

LADY	Foot Position	Alignment	Amount of Turn	Footwork	Count
1	RF to side	Backing wall	No turn	BF	1
2	LF behind RF without weight (Cuban Cross)	"	"	T (Pressure)	a
3	Take minimal weight to LF and replace weight to RF	"	"	BF	2

Other alignments may be used

Precedes	**(St)**	1-3 Natural Basic Movement - Reverse Basic Movement - Whisk to R - RF Samba Walk in PP turning 1/4 R (Lady L) as first step is taken to side - Volta travelling to L
	(A)	Criss Cross Voltas ended facing partner - Solo Spot Volta R (Lady L) - Reverse Turn ended facing wall - Corta Jaca
	(L)	Rolling of the Arm ended facing partner - Maypole (Man turning R)
	(F)	Reverse Roll ended facing wall - Promenade and Counter Promenade Runs (turn to face partner on 1 of Whisk)
Follows	**(St)**	Natural Basic Movement - Whisk to R - Volta travelling to L
	(A)	Solo Spot Volta to R (Lady to L) - Corta Jaca
	(L)	Argentine Crosses commenced with RF
	(F)	Natural Roll - Promenade and Counter Promenade Runs
Note	**Man and Lady**	
	(St,A,L&F)	When dancing a Whisk to L Man may lead Lady to turn R under raised L arm, releasing hold with R hand (Lady 1/4 turn R and RF fwd, then 2 and 3 of Spot Volta, L R, completing a further 3/4 to R). Regain normal hold at end of Lady's turn

WHISK TO RIGHT (ST,A,L&F)

Commence in Closed Position. Use Bounce action

MAN	Foot Position	Alignment	Amount of Turn	Foot-work	Lead	Count
1	RF to side	Facing wall	No turn	BF	Weight change	1
2	LF behind RF without weight (Cuban Cross)	"	"	T (Press-ure)	Retain tone in arms	a
3	Take minimal weight to LF and replace weight to RF	"	"	BF	Weight change	2

Other alignments may be used

LADY	Foot Position	Alignment	Amount of Turn	Footwork	Count
1	LF to side	Backing wall	No turn	BF	1
2	RF behind LF without weight (Cuban Cross)	"	"	T (Pressure)	a
3	Take minimal weight to RF and replace weight to LF	"	"	BF	2

Other alignments may be used

Precedes	**(St)**	Natural Basic Movement - 1-3 Reverse Basic Movement - Whisk to L - Volta Travelling to R
	(A)	Solo Spot Volta to L (Lady to R) - Foot Change 2 (from R Shadow Position to Closed Position)
	(L)	Maypole (Man turning L)
	(F)	Natural Roll
Follows	**(St)**	Reverse Basic Movement - Whisk to L - LF Samba Walk in PP (having turned to PP over 1-3 of Whisk)
	(A)	Bota Fogos to PP and CPP - Solo Spot Volta to L (Lady to R)
	(L&F)	Argentine Crosses
Note	**Man and Lady**	
	(St,A,L&F)	When dancing a Whisk to R Man may lead Lady to turn L under raised arm, releasing hold with R hand (Lady 1/4 turn L and LF fwd, then 2 and 3 of Spot Volta, R L, completing a further 3/4 L). Regain normal hold at end of Lady's turn

LEFT FOOT SAMBA WALK IN PROMENADE POSITION

Commence in Promenade Position, with feet pointing LOD. Use very slight Bounce action

MAN/ LADY	Foot Position	Alignment	Amount of Turn	Foot-work	Lead	Count
1	LF fwd in PP	Facing LOD	No turn	BF	Weight change	1
2	RF back in PP, without weight, small step. Toe turned out	Against LOD	"	I/E of T (Press-ure)	Retain tone in arms	a
3	Take minimal weight to RF and draw LF back about 8 cms (3 inches) in PP	"	"	F (Press-ure on ball of foot)	Weight change	2

SAMBA WALKS (continued)

RIGHT FOOT SAMBA WALK IN PROMENADE POSITION

MAN/ LADY	Foot Position	Alignment	Amount of Turn	Foot-work	Lead	Count
1	RF fwd in PP	Facing LOD	No turn	BF	Weight change	1
2	LF back in PP without weight, small step. Toe turned out	Against LOD	"	I/E of T (Press-ure)	Retain tone in arms	a
3	Take minimal weight to LF and draw RF back about 8 cms(3 inches) in PP	"	"	F (Press-ure on ball of foot)	Weight change	2

Notes **Man and Lady**

1   The very slight Bounce action combined with the foot positions causes the pelvis to swing naturally towards the stepping foot on 1 and 2 then commence to return to normal position on 3. This pelvic action is slight, not exaggerated

2   Because of the pelvic action the Samba Walks are danced with the lower part of the body facing LOD, with only the shoulders turned slightly towards partner creating the Promenade Position

3   Owing to the close proximity of the hips there is a slight adjustment of hold, Man sliding R hand to just belowLady's R shoulder blade, and Lady sliding L hand across Man's back at approximately shoulder blade level

4   On 3 the knee is slightly straightened as the foot is drawn back, then slightly flexed

SAMBA WALKS (continued)

Precedes to LF Samba Walk in Promenade Position

(St,A&L)	Whisk to R (having turned to PP over 1-3) - RF Samba Walk in PP - Side Samba Walk (turning 1/8 L, Lady R, on 1 of Samba Walk in PP)
(F)	Promenade and Counter Promenade Runs

Follows	**(St)**	RF Samba Walk in PP - Side Samba Walk
	(A,L&F)	4-9 Bota Fogos to PP & CPP

Precedes to RF Samba Walk in Promenade Position

(St)	LF Samba Walk in PP
(A)	Travelling Bota Fogos Back - Criss Cross Bota Fogos (with Lady's underarm turn ending in PP) - Bota Fogos to PP and CPP
(L)	Foot Change 4 (from R Shadow Position to PP)
(F)	Foot Change 6 (from R Contra Position to PP)

Follows **(St,A,L&F)** Whisk to L (turn 1/4 R on 1, Lady L, to face partner) - LF Samba Walk in PP

Note **(A,L&F)**

Samba Walks may be danced on same foot as partner when in R Shadow Position. They are also danced in RSP during Rolling off the Arm **(L&F)**

SIDE SAMBA WALK (ST,A,L&F)

Commence in Promenade Position. Use very slight Bounce action

MAN	Foot Position	Alignment	Amount of Turn	Foot-work	Lead	Count
1	RF fwd in PP	Facing LOD	No turn	BF	Weight change then slightly retract arms	1
2	LF to side and slightly back in PP without weight. Toe turned out	"	"	I/E of T (Pressure)	Increase tone in arms and slightly extend	a
3	Take minimal weight to LF and draw RF towards LF about 8 cms (3 inches) in PP	Facing DW	1/8 to R between 2 & 3	F (Pressure on ball of foot)	R arm to R side over 2 & 3	2

SIDE SAMBA WALK (continued)

LADY	Foot Position	Alignment	Amount of Turn	Footwork	Count
1	LF fwd in PP	Facing LOD	No turn	BF	1
2	RF to side and slightly back in PP without weight. Toe turned out	"	"	I/E of T (Pressure)	a
3	Take minimal weight to RF and draw LF towards RF about 8 cms (3 inches) in PP	Facing DC	1/8 to L between 2 & 3	F (Pressure on ball of foot)	2

Note   Man and Lady

Pelvic action and use of knees as Samba Walk in Promenade Position

Precedes	**(St)**	LF Samba Walk in PP
	(A)	Travelling Bota Fogos Back - Bota Fogos to PP & CPP
	(L)	Foot Change 4 (from R Shadow Position to PP)
	(F)	Foot Change 6 (from R Contra Position to PP)
Follow	**(St,A,L&F)**	LF Samba Walk in PP (first step fwd and slightly across)

SIDE SAMBA WALK

Alternative finishing positions and their follows

Open PP (having released hold with R hand)

(St)	Criss Cross Bota Fogos
(A)	Criss Cross Voltas - Solo Spot Volta to L (Lady to R)
(L&F)	Maypole (Man turning L) - Foot Change 3 (from Open PP to R Shadow Position)

Closed Position (having turned 1/4 R, Lady L, between 2 and 3)

(St&A)	Stationary Samba Walks
(L&F)	Argentine Crosses

STATIONARY SAMBA WALKS (ST,A,L&F)

Commence in Closed Position. Use very slight Bounce action

MAN	Foot Position	Alignment	Amount of Turn	Foot-work	Lead	Count
1	Close LF to RF	Facing wall	No turn	BF	Slightly retract arms	1
2	RF back without weight. Toe turned out	To centre	"	I/E of T (Press-ure)	Increase tone and slightly extend arms	a
3	Take minimal weight to RF and draw LF back about 8 cms(3 inches)	Backing centre	"	F (Press-ure on ball of foot	over 2 & 3	2
4	Close RF to LF slightly fwd	Facing wall	"	BF	Slightly retract arms	1
5	LF back without weight. Toe turned out	To centre	"	I/E of T (Press-ure)	Increase tone and slightly extend arms	a
6	Take minimal weight to LF and draw RF back about 8 cms (3 inches)	Backing centre	"	F (Press-ure on ball of foot	over 4 & 6	2

May be repeated, closing slightly forward on 1

STATIONARY SAMBA WALKS (continued)

LADY	Foot Position	Alignment	Amount of Turn	Footwork	Count
1	Close RF to LF	Facing centre	No turn	BF	1
2	LF back without weight. Toe turned out	To wall	"	I/E of T (Pressure)	a
3	Take minimal weight to LF and draw RF back about 8 cms (3 inches)	Backing wall	"	F (Pressure on ball of foot)	2
4	Close LF to RF slightly fwd	Facing centre	"	BF	1
5	RF back without weight. Toe turned out	To wall	"	I/E of T (Pressure)	a
6	Take minimal weight to RF and draw LF back about 8 cms (3 inches)	Backing wall	"	F (Pressure on ball of foot	2

May be repeated, closing slightly forward on 1

STATIONARY SAMBA WALKS (continued)

Notes	Man and Lady
1	Pelvic action and use of knees as Samba Walk in PP
2	Stationary Samba Walks may be danced with L to R hand hold

Precedes (St)   Side Samba Walk (Man 1/4 turn R, Lady L) -
Travelling Volta to L in Closed Position
(A)   Criss Cross Voltas (ended in Closed Position)
(L&F)   Maypole (Man turning R)

Precedes to 4-6 (RF Stationary Samba Walk)

(L&F)   Maypole (Man turning L)

Follows (St)   Reverse Basic Movement - Whisk to L
(A)   Bota Fogos to PP and CPP
(L&F)   Argentine Crosses - Maypole(Man turning L)

Follows to 1-3 (LF Stationary Samba Walk)

(St)   Natural Basic Movement - Whisk to R
(A)   Corta Jaca
(L)   Argentine Crosses commenced with RF -
Maypole (Man turning R)
(F)   Natural Roll

Note   Man and Lady

When dancing a LF Stationary Samba Walk Man may lead Lady to turn R under raised arms, having released hold with R hand (Lady Spot Volta making a complete turn to R)
Likewise, when dancing a RF Stationary Samba Walk Lady may be turned to L

NOTES

4   RHYTHM   BOUNCE (ST,A,L&F)

RHYTHM BOUNCE ON LEFT FOOT

Commence weight on either LF or RF.

Swing pelvis softly in the direction of the free leg	**Count "a"**
Swing pelvis softly in the direction of the standing leg	**Count "1"**

Repeat movement for the desired number of counts
To suit the musical phasing

1   The Rhythm Bounce may be commenced
     Maintaining both the weight on the standing leg and
     the foot position e.g. after any Boto Fogo action.

2   Maintaining the weight on the standing leg, moving
     the free leg to a side or diagonally back position
     e.g. after a whisk,

3   Dancing a weight change by stepping side or
     diagonally forward e.g. after a traveling volta
     (commence on count "1")

RHYTHM BOUNCE ON RIGHT FOOT

Precedes and Follows None are listed, as the principal use of the
Rhythum Bounce is to start the dance, or as a means of achieving
good phrasing or a foot change.
The Rhythm Bounce can be used in any position,

NOTES

5   VOLTA MOVEMENTS (ST,A,L&F)

There are three types of Volta Movements, namely, Travelling
Volta, Circular Volta and Spot Volta. Volta Movements may commence with either RF or LF, and are used in a variety of ways
throughout the Samba syllabus. The Alignment, Amount of Turn
and Lead for Volta Movements depend on the specific figure. The
charts below describe the basic foot placement for any Volta Movement, and would represent the Travelling Volta in Closed Position.

VOLTA COMMENCED WITH RIGHT FOOT

MAN / LADY	Foot Position	Footwork	Count
1	RF in front of LF (Cuban Cross)	BF	1
2	LF to side and slightly back without weight, toe turned out	Pressure on I/E of T	a
3	Take part weight to LF and draw RF in front of LF (Cuban Cross)	BF (Pressure on ball of foot)	2
4-7	Repeat steps 2 and 3 twice	As for 2 & 3	a 1 a 2

VOLTA COMMENCED WITH LEFT FOOT

MAN / LADY	Foot Position	Footwork	Count
1	LF in front of RF (Cuban Cross)	BF	1
2	RF to side and slightly back without weight, toe turned out	Pressure on I/E of T	a
3	Take part weight to RF and draw LF in front of RF (Cuban Cross)	BF (Pressure on ball of foot)	2
4-7	Repeat steps 2 and 3 twice	As for 2 & 3	a 1 a 2

VOLTA MOVEMENTS (continued)

Notes

1   The teaching count of "1 a 2 a 3 a 4" may be used

2   A Volta may be extended for an additional 1 or 2 bars of music, repeating steps 2 and 3 two or four times

3   **(L&F)**   When the Volta is commenced with RF a pelvic action may be used as follows: "Push" off ball of RF and move hips to right on the "a" counts. Return hips to normal position on the numerical count. (When commencing with LF push off ball of LF and move hips to left on the "a" counts)

TRAVELLING VOLTA (ST,A,L&F)

This Volta may be danced without turn. It will travel to left when commenced with RF, or to right when commenced with LF. In more advanced versions the Travelling Volta may turn up to approximately 3/8 left or right over two bars of music.

(St,A,L&F)   Travelling Volta to left commenced with RF (Lady LF) may be danced in Closed Position, without turn, moving along LOD (Man facing wall, Lady facing centre). Normal or left to right hand hold may be used

Precedes (St)   Rhythm Bounce on LF - Whisk to L
      (A&L)   Travelling Bota Fogos Back - Bota Fogo to PP
      (F)   Promenade and Counter Promenade Runs (commencing Volta with step 2)

Follow   **(St,A,L&F)** Whisk to Left

VOLTA MOVEMENTS (continued)

(St,A,L&F)   Travelling Volta to right commenced with LF (Lady RF) may be danced in Closed Position, without turn, moving along LOD (Man facing centre, Lady facing wall). Normal or left to right hand hold may be used

Precedes

(St,A,L&F)   Rhythm Bounce on RF - Whisk to R

Follow

(St,A,L&F)   Whisk to R

The Travelling Volta is also used in the following figures:-

(A,L&F)   Criss Cross Voltas (page 64) - Shadow Travelling Volta (page 78)

CIRCULAR VOLTA (L&F)

This is the Volta making up to approximately one complete turn to right or left over two bars of music. The front foot travels around the circumference of a small circle

The Circular Volta is used in the following figures :-

(L)   Maypole (Man) (page 116) - Shadow Circular Volta (page 118)

(F)   Roundabout (page 124)

VOLTA MOVEMENTS (continued)

THE SPOT VOLTA (ST,A,L&F)

This is the Volta making up to one complete turn over one bar of music. After the first step is placed, the ball of the front foot remains on the spot. Turn is made between steps 2 and 3 by swivelling on the ball of the front foot, then lowering the front heel as the Cuban Cross is achieved. In more advanced versions, up to two complete turns are made

The Spot Volta is used in the following figures :-

(St)	Lady 1-3 Spot Volta to right under raised arms (Man dances Whisk to L) - Lady 1-3 Spot Volta to left under raised arms (Man dances Whisk to R)
(A)	Solo Spot Volta (page 68)
(L&F)	Maypole (Lady)

Note	Lady dances 1-3 of Spot Volta turning to right under raised arms as an ending to the following figures:-
(St)	Criss Cross Bota Fogos (page 54)
(L&F)	Argentine Crosses (page 110)
(A)	Lady dances 1-3 of Spot Volta in Foot Changes 1 and 2, and **(L&F)** Foot Changes 3 and 4 (see page 74)

Inclination of body

A slight inclination of body to the right may be used when the Volta is commenced with RF, or to left when commenced with LF. The degree of inclination may be gradually increased in proportion to the amount of turn used

VOLTA MOVEMENTS (continued)

Exceptions

No inclination of body is used in the Maypole, or when Lady is
dancing her Spot Volta turning under arm, or during a Foot
Change. In the Roundabout, when commenced with RF, Man may
incline his body slightly to right or left (Lady normal opposite).
Likewise, when commenced with LF, the body may be inclined
either way. The inclination of the body is not increased

Development   (F)

When Travelling Volta is danced without turn in Closed Position, or
when in Shadow Position, a more advanced timing may be used
taking the first step on count "1 and",then hold position for "2 and",
then continue with steps 2 - 5 for counts "a 3 a 4"

The Bounce action in detail is described below:-
Commence with knees slightly flexed, weight on LF, after the count
of "2 and"

	Count
As RF commences to move into position commence the	
upward part of Bounce	a
Arrive up	1
Commence downward part of Bounce	and
Continue to go down	2
Arrive down	and

Continue as normal " a 1 a 2"
(Lady normal opposite)

Syllabus Requirements for Student Teacher examinations

Travelling Volta in Closed Position
As Lady, 1-3 Spot Volta under arm as Man dances a Whisk, or as
described under Follows to Criss Cross Bota Fogos

NOTES

Commence in Closed Position. Use Bounce action

MAN	Foot Position	Alignment	Amount of Turn	Foot-work	Lead	Count
1	RF fwd in CBMP, OP	Facing DC	No turn	BF	Weight change	1
2	LF to side without weight	Toe pointing DC. Body facing LOD	1/4 to R over 2 & 3	I/E of T (Press-ure)	Retain tone in arms	a
3	Take minimal weight to LF and replace weight to RF	Facing DW		BF	Weight change	2
4	LF fwd in CBMP,OP on L side	"	No turn	BF	"	1
5	RF to side without weight	Toe pointing DW. Body facing LOD	1/4 to L over 5 & 6	I/E of T (Press-ure)	Retain tone in arms	a
6	Take minimal weight to RF and replace weight to LF	Facing DC		BF	Weight change	2

1-6 may be repeated

TRAVELLING BOTA FOGOS FORWARD (continued)

LADY	Foot Position	Alignment	Amount of Turn	Footwork	Count
1	LF back in CBMP	Backing DC	No turn	BF	1
2	RF to side without weight	RF backing DW. Body backing LOD	1/4 to R over 2 & 3	I/E of T (Pressure)	a
3	Take minimal weight to RF and replace weight to LF	Backing DW		BF	2
4	RF back in CBMP	Backing DW	No turn	BF	1
5	LF to side without weight	LF backing DC. Body backing LOD	1/4 to L over 5 & 6	I/E of T (Pressure)	a
6	Take minimal weight to LF and replace weight to RF	Backing DC		BF	2

1-6 may be repeated

Note Man and Lady

(A,L&F) Travelling Bota Fogos Fwd may be danced on same foot as partner when in R Shadow Position

Same Foot Bota Fogo to Contra Position

(F) A "same foot" Bota Fogo commenced with LF may be turned 1/8 or 1/4 to L, leading Lady to turn strongly to L towards end of first step,then releasing hold (Lady turn 5/8 or 3/4 to L). End in R Contra Position taking normal hold

A "same foot" Bota Fogo commenced with RF may be danced in the same manner, turning to R to end in L Contra Position
Follow with Contra Bota Fogos or Roundabout

Precedes (St,A,L&F)   Natural Basic Movement commenced facing LOD (Turn 1/8 L over 2 and 3. 4-6 are danced with Lady outside)

To step 4 Commence in line with Lady

(St)	1-3 Natural Basic Movement - Reverse Basic Movement
(A&L)	Reverse Turn
(F)	Reverse Roll

Follow (St,A,L&F)   Natural Basic Movement commenced OP (Turn 1/8 R over 2 and 3 to face partner)

NOTES

7 CRISS CROSS BOTA FOGOS (SHADOW BOTA FOGOS) (ST,A,L&F)

Commence in Open Promenade Position.   L to R hand hold.   Use Bounce action

MAN	Foot Position	Alignment	Amount of Turn	Foot-work	Lead	Count
1-3	Travelling Bota Fogo Fwd LRL. End in Open CPP	Commence facing DW. End facing DC	1/4 to L over 2 & 3	As Travel-ling Bota Fogos Fwd	Raise L arm and move it very slightly to L	1 a 2
4-6	Travelling Bota Fogo Fwd RLR. End in Open PP	End facing DW	1/4 to R over 5 & 6	"	Move L arm very slightly to R	1 a 2

1-3 or 1-6 may be repeated

LADY	Foot Position	Alignment	Amount of Turn	Footwork	Count
1-3	Travelling Bota Fogo Fwd RLR, passing in front of Man under raised arms. End in Open CPP	Commence facing DC. End facing DW	1/4 to R over 2 & 3	As Travelling Bota Fogos Fwd	1a 2
4-6	Travelling Bota Fogo Fwd LRL, passing in front of Man under raised arms. End in Open PP	End facing DC	1/4 to L over 5 & 6	"	1 a 2

1-3 or 1-6 may be repeated

Precedes (St)		Side Samba Walk (leading Lady slightly in advance on 1)
	(A,L&F)	Criss Cross Voltas

Precede to 4 - 6

	(A&L)	1-7 Criss Cross Voltas
	(F)	Foot Change 7 (R Contra Position to Open CPP) - Samba Locks

Follows	**(St)**	* LF Stationary Samba Walk leading Lady to turn R under raised arms (Lady 1-3 Spot Volta turning 3/4 R). Regain hold and follow with Natural or Progressive Basic Movement **(A&L)** Corta Jaca **(F)** Natural Roll
	(A)	Criss Cross Voltas
	(L&F)	Maypole (Man turning L) - Foot Change 3 (Open PP to R Shadow Position)

Follows to step 3

	(A)	8-14 Criss Cross Voltas
	(L)	Maypole (Man turning R)
	(F)	Samba Locks

Alternative finishing positions for the LF Stationary Walk with Lady's underarm turn

Promenade Position (A,L&F)
Man turn 1/8 L on Stationary Samba Walk and Lady 1 1/8 R on Spot Volta to end facing LOD, both turning body a little less to shape the Promenade Position. Regain normal hold to follow with a RF Samba Walk in PP or a Side Samba Walk

Right Side Position (L&F)
Amount of turn as above but with body also facing LOD on last step. Lower joined hands to just above waist level in front of the bodies. Lady's L hand well across her body at waist level, the Man's R hand behind her back, taking her L hand in his R hand (Double hold)
Follow with a RF Samba Walk into Rolling off the Arm

8   TRAVELLING BOTA FOGOS BACK (A,L&F)

Commence in Closed Position. Use Bounce action

MAN	Foot Position	Alignment	Amount of Turn	Foot-work	Lead	Count
1	RF back	Backing DW	No turn	BF	Weight change	1
2	LF to side without weight	LF backing DC. Body backing LOD	1/4 to L over 2 & 3	I/E of T (Press-ure)	Retain tone in arms	a
3	Take minimal weight to LF and replace to RF	Backing DC		BF	Weight change	2
4	LF back in CBMP	Backing DC	No turn	BF	"	1
5	RF to side without weight	RF backing DW. Body backing LOD	1/4 to R over 5 & 6	I/E of T (Press-ure)	Retain tone in arms	a
6	Take minimal weight to RF and replace weight to LF	Backing DW		BF	Weight change	2

MAN	Foot Position	Alignment	Amount of Turn	Foot-work	Lead	Count
7	RF back in CBMP	Backing LOD	1/8 to L	BF	"	1
8	LF to side without weight	LF pointing DW. Body backing centre	3/8 to L over 8 & 9	I/E of T (Press-ure)	Retain tone in arms	a
9	Take minimal weight to LF and replace weight to RF	Backing DC against LOD		BF	Weight change	2
10	LF back in CBMP	Against LOD	1/8 to L	BF	Weight change	1
11	RF back without weight. Toe turned out	" "	No turn	I/E of T (Press-ure)	With R hand comm-ence to turn Lady to PP	a
12	Take minimal weight to RF and replace weight to LF in PP	LF pointing to LOD	Slight body turn to L	BF	Conti-nue to turn Lady to PP	2

TRAVELLING BOTA FOGOS BACK (continued)

LADY	Foot Position	Alignment	Amount of Turn	Footwork	Count
1	LF fwd	Facing DW	No turn	BF	1
2	RF to side without weight	Toe pointing DW. Body facing LOD	1/4 to L over 2 & 3	I/E of T (Pressure)	a
3	Take minimal weight to RF and replace weight to LF	Facing DC		BF	2
4	RF fwd in CBMP, OP	"	No turn	BF	1
5	LF to side without weight	Toe pointing DC. Body facing LOD	1/4 to R over 5 & 6	I/E of T (Pressure)	a
6	Take minimal weight to LF and replace weight to RF	Facing DW		BF	2
7	LF fwd in CBMP, OP on L side	Facing LOD	1/8 to L	BF	1
8	RF to side without weight	Facing centre	3/8 to L over 8 & 9	I/E of T (Pressure)	a
9	Take minimal weight to RF and replace weight to LF	Facing DC against LOD		BF	2

TRAVELLING BOTA FOGOS BACK (continued)

LADY	Foot Position	Alignment	Amount of Turn	Footwork	Count
10	RF fwd in CBMP, OP	Facing against LOD	1/8 to L	BF	1
11	LF to side without weight	Toe pointing DC against LOD. Body facing centre	1/2 to R over 11 & 12 Body turns slightly less	I/E of T (Pressure)	a
12	Take minimal weight to LF and replace weight to RF in PP	RF pointing to LOD		BF	2

Precedes (A&L)   1-3 Reverse Turn
     (F)   1-3 Reverse Roll

Follows   (A&L)   RF Samba Walk in PP - Side Samba Walk -
Travelling Volta to L commenced with RF (Lady LF), turning to face partner on first step - 4-9 Bota Fogos to PP and CPP
     (F)   Foot Change 5 (PP to R Contra Position)

Commence in Closed Position. Use Bounce action

MAN	Foot Position	Alignment	Amount of Turn	Foot-work	Lead	Count
1	LF fwd	Facing wall	No turn	BF	Weight change	1
2	RF to side without weight	Pointing DW against LOD. Body facing wall	1/8 to L over 2 & 3	I/E of T (Press-ure)	Retain tone in arms	a
3	Take minimal weight to RF and replace weight to LF in PP	Facing DW		BF	Turn Lady to PP with press-ure through R hand	2
4	RF fwd and across in PP and CBMP	Moving along LOD, facing DW	No turn	BF	Weight change	1
5	LF to side without weight	Pointing DW. Body facing wall	1/4 to R over 5 & 6	I/E of T (Press-ure)	Turn Lady to L with press-ure through R hand	a
6	Take minimal weight to LF and replace weight to RF in CPP	Facing DW against LOD		BF	Conti-nue to turn Lady to CPP	2

BOTA FOGOS TO PROMENADE AND COUNTER PROMENADE POSITION (continued)

MAN	Foot Position	Alignment	Amount of Turn	Foot-work	Lead	Count
7	LF fwd and across in CPP and CBMP	Moving against LOD, facing DW against LOD	No turn	BF	Weight change	1
8	RF to side without weight	Pointing DW against LOD. Body facing wall	3/8 to L over 8 & 9. Body turns slightly less	I/E of T (Pressure)	Turn Lady to R with pressure through R hand	a
9	Take minimal weight to RF and replace weight to LF in PP	Facing LOD		BF	Continue to turn Lady to PP	2

BOTA FOGOS TO PROMENADE AND COUNTER PROMENADE POSITION (continued)

LADY	Foot Position	Alignment	Amount of Turn	Footwork	Count
1	RF back	Backing wall	No turn	BF	1
2	LF to side without weight	Pointing DC against LOD. Body facing centre	1/8 to R over 2 & 3	I/E of T (Pressure)	a
3	Take minimal weight to LF and replace weight to RF in PP	Facing DC		BF	2
4	LF fwd and across in PP and CBMP	Moving along LOD, facing DC	No turn	BF	1
5	RF to side without weight	Pointing DC. Body facing centre	1/4 to L over 5 & 6	I/E of T (Pressure)	a
6	Take minimal weight to RF and replace weight to LF in CPP	Facing DC against LOD		BF	2

BOTA FOGOS TO PROMENADE AND COUNTER PROMENADE POSITION (continued)

LADY	Foot Position	Alignment	Amount of Turn	Footwork	Count
7	RF fwd and across in CPP and CBMP	Moving against LOD, facing DC against LOD	No turn	BF	1
8	LF to side without weight	Pointing DC against LOD. Body facing centre	3/8 to R over 8 & 9. Body turns slightly less	I/E of T (Pressure)	a
9	Take minimal weight to LF and replace weight to RF in PP	Facing LOD		BF	2

Precedes (A&L)   1-3 Natural Basic Movement - Reverse Basic Movement - Whisk to R - Stationary Samba Walks - Reverse Turn (ended facing wall)

      (F)   Reverse Roll (ended facing wall)

Precedes to 4- 9

     (A,L&F)   LF Samba Walk in PP - Travelling Bota Fogos Back

Follows (A&L)   RF Samba Walk in PP - Side Samba Walk - Travelling Volta to L commenced with RF (Lady LF) turning to face partner on first step

      (F)   Foot Change 5 (from PP to R Contra Position) having made 1/4 turn over 8 & 9

Note   **Man and Lady**

A Bota Fogo to PP may be danced (steps 1-3 only)

Commence in Open Promenade Position. L to R hand hold. Use
Bounce action

MAN	Foot Position	Alignment	Amount of Turn	Foot-work	Lead	Count
1-7	Dance 2 bars of Travelling Volta to R, curving to L behind Lady's back. End in Open CPP LRLRLRL	Commence facing DW. End facing DC	1/4 to L over 1-7	As Volta	Raise L arm and gradu-ally move it to L to lead Lady to pass in front and to L side. Lower arm slightly over 4-7	1 a 2 a 1 a 2
8-14	Dance 2 bars of Travelling Volta to L, curving to R behind Lady's back, to end facing her in Closed Position RLRLRLR	End facing wall	3/8 to R over 8-14	"	Raise L arm and gradu-ally move it to R to lead Lady to pass in front. Lower arm slightly over 8-14 to return to normal position	1 a 2 a 1 a 2

CRISS CROSS VOLTAS (continued)

LADY	Foot Position	Alignment	Amount of Turn	Footwork	Count
1-7	Dance 2 bars of Travelling Volta to L, curving to R passing in front of Man. End in Open CPP RLRLRLR	Commence facing DC. End facing DW	1/4 to R over 1-7	As Volta	1 a 2 a 1 a 2
8-14	Dance 2 bars of Travelling Volta to R, curving to L passing in front of Man to end facing him in Closed Position LRLRLRL	End facing centre	3/8 to L over 8-14	"	1 a 2 a 1 a 2

Precedes (A,L&F)   Side Samba Walk (leading Lady slightly in advance on 1, or moving slightly in advance of Lady and passing in front of her over steps 1-7 of the Criss Cross Voltas) - Criss Cross Bota Fogos

Precedes to 8-14

      (A&L)   1-3 Criss Cross Bota Fogos
      (F)   Foot Change 7 (R Contra Position to Open CPP) - Samba Locks

Follows   (A)   Reverse Basic Movement - Whisk to L - Stationary Samba Walks - Bota Fogos to PP and CPP
      (L&F)   Argentine Crosses

CRISS CROSS VOLTAS (continued)

Follows when ended in Open PP (1/4 turn over 8-14)

(A)	Criss Cross Bota Fogos
(L&F)	Maypole (Man turning L) - Foot Change 3 (Open PP to R Shadow Position)

Follows when ended in Open CPP (having danced 1-7 of Criss Cross Voltas)

(A)	4-6 Criss Cross Bota Fogos
(L)	Maypole (Man turning R)
(F)	Samba Locks

Follow when ended in Right Side Position (having turned 1/8 R, Lady 1/8 L, over 8-14 to face LOD) and taken Double hand hold as for Rolling off the Arm

(L&F)	Two Samba Walks in RSP commenced with LF (Lady RF) and then Rolling off the Arm, or omit the Walks and follow immediately with Rolling off the Arm

Note   Man and Lady

6 & 7 may be danced as 2 & 3 of a Bota Fogo (Man turning L and Lady R) 13 & 14 may be danced as 2 & 3 of a Bota Fogo (Man turning R and Lady L). Amount of turn remains unchanged

NOTES

Commence in Open Position L to R hand hold. Use Bounce action

MAN	Foot Position	Alignment	Amount of Turn	Foot-work	Lead	Count
1	LF in front of RF (Cuban Cross)	Commence facing wall and turn to face centre	1/2 to L	BF	Move L hand slightly to L to turn Lady to R, then release hold	1
2	RF to side and slightly back without weight Toe turned out	Towards alignment of 3	1/2 to L over 2 & 3	I/E of T (Press-ure)	No lead	a
3	Take part weight to RF and swivel on ball of LF keeping it in place. End LF in front of RF (Cuban Cross) in Closed Position	Facing wall		BF	Regain requir-ed hold at end of turn	2

Note

1   On 3 L heel lowers at end of turn

2   The Solo Spot Volta may be turned to R (Lady to L). Man's steps as Lady's chart

3   An additional bar of music may be used by repeating 2 & 3 twice, completing another full turn to L, count "a 1 a 2" (or use teaching count "a 3 a 4")

SOLO SPOT VOLTA (continued)

LADY	Foot Position	Alignment	Amount of Turn	Footwork	Count
1	RF in front of LF (Cuban Cross)	Commence facing centre and turn to face wall	1/2 to R	BF	1
2	LF to side and slightly back without weight Toe turned out	Towards alignment of 3	1/2 to R over 2 & 3	I/E of T (Pressure)	a
3	Take part weight to LF and swivel on ball of RF keeping it in place. End RF in front of LF (Cuban Cross) in Closed Position	Facing centre		BF	2

Note

1   On 3 R heel lowers at end of turn

2   The Solo Spot Volta may be turned the other way (Man turn R, Lady L). Lady's steps as Man's chart

3   An additional bar of music may be used by repeating 2 & 3 twice, completing another full turn to R, count "a 1 a 2" (or use the teaching count "a 3 a 4")

4   1 complete turn can be used over two bars of music

SOLO SPOT VOLTA (continued)

Precedes to Solo Spot Volta to Left

(A,L&F)	Whisk to R - Side Samba Walk (1/4 turn) - RF Stationary Walk - Solo Spot Volta to R (Lady to L) - Corta Jaca

Follows	**(A)**	Whisk to R - RF Stationary Walk - Solo Spot Volta to R (Lady to L)
	(L)	Argentine Crosses commenced with RF
	(F)	Promenade and Counter Promenade Runs

Solo Spot Volta to Left may commence in Open PP Turn 7/8 L (Lady 7/8 R) on the Spot Volta

Precede **(A,L&F)** Side Samba Walk

Precedes to Solo Spot Volta to Right

(A,L&F)	Whisk to L - LF Stationary Walk - Solo Spot Volta to L (Lady to R)

Follows	**(A)**	Whisk to L - LF Stationary Walk - Solo Spot Volta to L (Lady to R)
	(L&F)	Argentine Crosses

(F) Solo Spot Volta to Right may commence in Open CPP Turn 7/8 R (Lady 7/8 L) on the Spot Volta

Precede **(F)** Forward Locks

NOTES

12   FOOT CHANGES (A,L&F)

Certain figures in Samba maybe danced in Right Shadow Position or Contra Position requiring Man and Lady to use the same foot. In every case the change of foot is achieved by the Man, the Lady dancing three steps to the counts of "1 a 2 "

Figures that may be danced in Right Shadow Position are :-

(A)   Samba Walks - Travelling Bota Fogos Fwd - Shadow Travelling Voltas = Rhythm Bounce

(L)   Shadow Circular Voltas

(F)   Cruzados Walks and Locks

Man and Lady dance the Man's steps with normal technique although alignments are flexible

Any amalgamation of the above figures is acceptable

Man uses minimal Bounce action when dancing the Foot Changes

Foot Changes required for the theoretical section of the Professional examinations are listed on next pages. Other methods are acceptable in the practical section and in medal tests

1 (A,L&F) CLOSED POSITION TO RIGHT SHADOW POSITION

Precede with any figure ended in Closed Position with weight on LF (Lady RF). Alignment depends on preceding figure

MAN	Count
Replace weight to RF leading Lady to turn L and releasing hold	1
Hold position with weight on RF	a
LF diagonally fwd, small step	2
Take R Shadow hold at end of Lady's turn	

(Alternatively, turn Lady under raised L arm and then change to R Shadow hold)

LADY 1-3 of Spot Volta turning 1/2 L (LRL)

Follow with a figure commenced with RF

2 (A,L&F) RIGHT SHADOW TO CLOSED POSITION

Precede with a figure danced in R Shadow Position and ended with weight on LF. Alignment depends on preceding figure

MAN	Count
RF fwd, leading Lady to turn R and releasing hold	1
Hold position with weight on RF	a
Turn 1/4 R on RF and close LF to RF	2
Take normal hold at end of Lady's turn	

LADY 1-3 of Spot Volta turning 3/4 R (RLR)

Follow with any figure commenced in Closed Position starting with RF (Lady LF) ,depending on alignment

3   **(A,L&F) PROMENADE OR OPEN PROMENADE POSITION TO RIGHT SHADOW POSITION**

Precede with a Side Samba Walk, Criss Cross Bota Fogos or Criss Cross Voltas (ended Man facing DW, Lady facing DC)

MAN	**Count**
LF fwd, leading Lady to turn R and releasing hold	1
Hold position with weight on LF	a
RF to side and slightly fwd	2
Take R Shadow hold at end of Lady's turn	

(Alternatively turn Lady under raised L arm and then change to R Shadow Hold)

LADY 1.2 of Spot Volta turning R, then continue to turn R on LF to end RF to side and slightly fwd, facing DW, having completed 1 1/4 turns

Follow with a figure commenced with LF or both step LF fwd DW (Count "1") and RF to side and slightly fwd, knee slightly flexed (Count "2") then continue as above

4   **(L&F) RIGHT SHADOW POSITION TO PROMENADE POSITION**

Precede with a figure danced in R Shadow Position and ended with weight on LF, facing LOD

MAN	**Count**
RF fwd, small step, leading Lady to turn R and releasing hold	1
Hold position with weight on RF	a
LF fwd, small step, achieving normal hold in PP	2

LADY 1.2 of Spot Volta turning R (RL) then continue to turn R on LF and RF fwd in PP, completing a full turn

Follow with a RF Samba Walk in PP or Side Samba Walk

5   **(F) PROMENADE POSITION TO RIGHT CONTRA POSITION**

Precede with a Bota Fogo to PP (ended Man facing DW, Lady facing DC)

Man leads Lady to dance a Bota Fogo turning 1/4 L (LRL) while he dances one of the following methods, all ended in R Contra Position

	Count
a) **Point Fwd and Back**	
Point RF fwd in PP without weight (Toe)	1
Hold position with weight on LF	a
Point RF diagonally back without weight (I/E of Toe)	2
b) **Rock Fwd and Back**	
RF fwd in PP	1
Hold position with weight on RF	a
Replace weight back to LF	2
c) **Double Rock**	
RF fwd in PP	1
Replace LF back, without weight (Toe)	a
Take minimal weight to LF and replace weight fwd to RF	2
Replace LF back without weight (Toe)	a
Take minimal weight to LF when taking first step of following figure	
d) **Flick Ball Change**	
Flick RF fwd in PP, slightly off floor	1
RF diag back without weight (I/E of Toe)	a
Take minimal weight to RF and replace weight fwd to LF	2

Follow all methods with a RF Contra Bota Fogo or Roundabout turning R

6   **RIGHT CONTRA POSITION TO PROMENADE POSITION**

Precede with a LF Contra Bota Fogo ended facing DW (Lady facing DC against LOD). Man leads Lady to dance a Bota Fogo turning 1/4 R (RLR) while he dances any one of the four methods described for Foot Change 5 above

Follow with a RF Samba Walk in PP or Side Samba Walk making a slight turn L (Lady R) as first step is danced

7   (F) RIGHT CONTRA POSITION TO OPEN COUNTER PROMENADE POSITION

Precede with a LF Contra Bota Fogo (ended Man facing DW, Lady facing DC against LOD)

MAN   **Count**

Two Stationary Samba Walks (RLR LRL)   1 a 2   1 a 2
gradually turning 1/4 L to face DC, raising
L arm and leading Lady into 1-7 of Criss
Cross Voltas behind back
End in Open CPP

LADY

1-7 of Criss Cross Voltas passing behind   1 a 2 a 1 a 2
Man's back to his L side and curving 1/2
R to end in Open CPP, facing DW (RLRLRLR)

Follow with 4 -6 Criss Cross Bota Fogos, 8-14 Criss
Cross Voltas, Maypole (Man turning R) or Samba Locks

8   (L,F)   FROM RIGHT SIDE POSITION TO RIGHT SHADOW POSITION

Precede with 1-3 of Rolling off the Arm

MAN   **Count**

RF to side, small step. With R hand lead   1
Lady to turn L and to move DC
Hold position with weight on RF, continuing   a
to turn Lady strongly L then release hold
with R hand
LF to side and slightly fwd, turning 1/8 L to   2
face DC taking R Shadow hold

(Note Place R hand on Lady's back at the beginning of
third step so Lady may follow the weight change. Take L
to L hand hold at end of step)

LADY   LF fwd (1/8 L to face DC)   1
Turning 3/8 L on LF, RF side, backing LOD   2
Turning 5/8 L on RF, LF side and slightly   3
fwd, facing DC

Follow with a figure commenced with RF

NOTES

This is a Travelling Volta danced in R Shadow Position, Man and Lady using the same foot. It may commence with RF, moving to L, curving up to 3/8 R over 1-7, or commenced with LF, moving to R and curving up to 3/8 L (teaching count "1 a 2 a 3 a 4"). The Travelling Volta may be continued for one or two additional bars of music

Precedes to Travelling Volta commenced with RF

(A&L)	Foot Change 1 (Closed Position to R Shadow Position)
(F)	Foot Change 8 (RSP to R Shadow Position)

Precedes when already in R Shadow Position, using same foot as partner

(A)	LF Samba Walk - LF Travelling Bota Fogo Fwd - Shadow Travelling Volta commenced with LF
(L)	Shadow Circular Volta commenced with LF
(F)	Cruzado Walks or Locks ended with weight on LF

Follows (all on same foot as partner)

(A)	LF Samba Walk - LF Travelling Bota Fogo Fwd - Shadow Travelling Volta commenced with LF
(L)	Shadow Circular Volta commenced with LF
(F)	"Same Foot" Bota Fogo to R Contra Position - Cruzado Walks or Locks commenced with LF

Note
The last two steps of Shadow Travelling Volta may be replaced with 2 & 3 of a Bota Fogo. Amount of turn remains unchanged

SHADOW TRAVELLING VOLTA (continued)

Precedes to Travelling Volta commenced with LF

(L&F)   Foot Change 3 (PP or Open PP to R Shadow Position)

Precedes when already in R Shadow Position (all on same foot as partner)

(A)   RF Samba Walk - RF Travelling Bota Fogo Fwd - Shadow Travelling Volta commenced with RF

(L)   Shadow Circular Volta commenced with RF

(F)   Cruzado Walks or Locks ended with weight on RF

Follows **(A)**   Foot Change 2 (R Shadow Position to Closed Position)

        (L&F)   Foot Change 4 (R Shadow Position to PP)

Follows (all on same foot as partner)

(A)   RF Samba Walk - RF Travelling Bota Fogo Fwd - Shadow Travelling Volta commenced with RF

(L)   Shadow Circular Volta commenced with RF

(F)   "Same Foot" Bota Fogo to R Contra Position - Cruzado Walks or Locks commenced with RF

Developments (L&F)

After 2 bars of Travelling Volta continue with 2 bars of Circular Volta or vice versa. Teaching count "1 a 2 a 3 a 4 a 5 a 6 a 7 a 8"

Commence in Closed Position. Use Bounce action

MAN	Foot Position	Alignment	Amount of Turn	Foot-work	Lead	Count
1	LF fwd	Commence facing LOD and turn to face DC	1/8 to L	BF	Weight change	1
2	RF to side and slightly back, without weight	Backing wall	1/8 to L between 1 & 2	I/E of T (Press-ure)	Retain tone in arms	a
3	Take minimal weight to RF and cross LF in front of RF. Toe turned out	Backing DW	1/8 to L between 2 & 3	BF	Weight change	2
4	RF back and slightly rightwards	Backing DC	1/4 to L between 3 & 4	BF	"	1
5	Place L heel close to R heel, without weight	Pointing DW	1/4 to L between 4 & 5. Body turns less	B (Press-ure)	Retain tone in arms	a
6	Take minimal weight to LF and close RF to LF	Facing DW	Body completes turn	BF	Weight change	2

May be repeated
Inclination of Body
  1   Slightly fwd
  2.3   Fwd and slightly L
  4   Slightly back
  6.7   Back and slightly R

REVERSE TURN (continued)

Notes   Man

1   When following with another Reverse Turn step 1 is facing
     LOD. Turn 1/4 L between 1 and 2 to back wall, then con-
     tinue as chart. (A complete turn is made overall)

2   The timing of   S Q Q S Q Q may be used, causing the
     following differences:-
     Full weight is taken on to each step
     Footwork on 2 B and on 5 BF
     There is no Bounce action

LADY	Foot Position	Alignment	Amount of Turn	Footwork	Count
1	RF back	Commence backing LOD and turn to back DC	1/8 to L	BF	1
2	Place L heel close to R heel, without weight	Pointing DW	1/4 to L between 1 & 2. Body turns less	B (Pressure)	a
3	Take minimal weight to LF and close RF to LF	Facing DW	Body completes turn	BF	2
4	LF fwd	Facing LOD	1/8 to L between 3 & 4	BF	1
5	RF to side and slightly back, without weight	Backing wall	1/4 to L between 4 & 5	I/E of T (Pressure)	a
6	Take minimal weight to RF and cross LF in front of RF. Toe turned out	Backing DW	1/8 to L between 5 & 6	BF	2

May be repeated

Inclination of body

1	Slightly back
2.3	Back and slightly R
4	Slightly fwd
5.6	Fwd and slightly L

REVERSE TURN (continued)

Notes   **Lady**

1   When following with another Reverse Turn there is a
1/4 turn L between preceding step and 1. Foot position
on 1 will be RF back and slightly rightwards. Continue
as chart. (A complete turn is made overall)

2   The timing of S Q Q S Q Q may be used, causing the
following differences
Full weight is taken on to each step
Footwork on 2 BF and on 5 B
There is no Bounce action

Precedes (A)   1-3 Natural Basic Movement - Reverse Basic
Movement - Reverse Turn - 1-3 Closed Rocks

    (L)   1-3 Open Rocks - Rolling off the Arm (Lady
overturned to Closed Position) - Maypole
(Man turning R)

    (F)   Reverse Roll

Precedes to step 4

    (L&F)   Back Rocks - Plait

Follows   **(A&L)**   Reverse Basic Movement - Whisk to L
(Reverse Turn underturned to end facing
wall) - Travelling Bota Fogo Fwd commenced
with LF - Bota Fogo to PP& CPP (Reverse
Turn underturned to end facing wall) -
Reverse Turn

    (F)   Reverse Roll

From step 3

    (A)   Travelling Bota Fogos Back

    (L&F)   Back Rocks - Plait

15 CORTA JACA (A,L&F)

Commence in Closed Position. No bounce

MAN	Foot Position	Alignment	Amount of Turn	Foot-work	Lead	Count
1	RF fwd, strong step	Facing wall	No turn	HF	Increase tone in arms and extend slightly fwd	S
2	LF fwd and slightly to side	"	"	H	Weight change. Retain arm position	Q
3	Slide RF leftwards	"	"	F (Pressure on ball of foot)	"	Q
4	LF back and slightly to side	Backing centre	"	B	"	Q
5	Slide RF leftwards	"	"	F (Pressure on ball of foot)	"	Q
6	LF fwd and slightly to side	Facing wall	"	H	"	Q
7	Slide RF leftwards	"	"	F (Pressure on ball of foot)	"	Q

CORTA JACA (continued)

LADY	Foot Position	Alignment	Amount of Turn	Footwork	Count
1	LF back	Backing wall	No turn	BF	S
2	RF back and slightly to side	"	"	B	Q
3	Slide LF rightwards	"	"	F (Pressure on ball of foot)	Q
4	RF fwd and slightly to side	Facing centre	"	H	Q
5	Slide LF rightwards	"	"	F (Pressure on ball of foot)	Q
6	RF back and slightly to side	Backing wall	"	B	Q
7	Slide LF rightwards	"	"	F (Pressure on ball of foot)	Q

Notes   **Man and Lady**

1   4-7 may be repeated

2   The toe is not lowered on 2 & 6 for the Man or (on 4 for the Lady)

CORTA JACA (continued)

Precedes (A)   Natural Basic Movement - 1-3 Reverse Basic Movement - Progressive Basic Movement - Whisk to L - LF Stationery Samba Walk - Lady's underarm turn ending to Criss Cross Bota Fogo - Closed Rocks (near corner)

          (L)   Lady's underarm turn ending to Argentine Crosses (near corner) - Maypole (Man turning L)

          (F)   Natural Roll

Follows   (A&L)   4-6 Natural Basic Movement - Solo Spot Volta to L (Lady to R)

          (F)   4-6 Natural Roll

Notes   Man and Lady

1		On 2-7 the R leg (Lady L leg) remains slightly flexed and L leg (Lady R leg) swings freely from the hip. Movement is felt mainly from the knee
2		The Corta Jaca may commence facing DW. Turn 1/8 R over steps 1-3
3	**(L)**	After step 7 Man may dance 1-7 of Lady's Corta Jaca while Lady dances Man's steps. Follow with Natural Basic Movement or Whisk to R
4	**(F)**	As note 3 turning up to 3/4 to R. Follow with any figure comenced with RF, depending on alignment

NOTES

Commence in Closed Position. No Bounce

MAN	Foot Position	Alignment	Amount of Turn	Foot-work	Lead	Count
1	RF fwd	Facing LOD	No turn	BF	Weight change, increasing tone in arms	S
2	LF fwd, small step	"	"	BF	Weight change, exerting slight pressure through L hand	Q
3	Replace weight to RF, toe slightly turned out	Against LOD	"	B	Weight change, retaining tone in arms	Q
4	LF fwd	Facing LOD	"	BF	"	S
5	RF fwd, small step	"	"	BF	Weight change, exerting slight pressure on Lady's back through fingers of R hand	Q
6	Replace weight to LF, toe slightly turned out	Against LOD	"	B	Weight change, retaining tone in arms	Q

CLOSED ROCKS (continued)

Notes Man

1   Steps 1-3 or 1-6 may be repeated

2   If preferred the back foot may be drawn slightly towards front foot on 3 and 6

CLOSED ROCKS (continued)

LADY	Foot Position	Alignment	Amount of Turn	Footwork	Count
1	LF back	Backing LOD	No turn	BF	S
2	RF back, small step, toe turned out. Knee slightly flexed	Down LOD, RF backing DW	1/8 to R (RF)	B	Q
3	Replace weight to LF	Facing against LOD	No turn	BF	Q
4	RF back	Backing LOD	1/8 to L (RF)	BF	S
5	LF back, small step, toe turned out. Knee slightly flexed	Down LOD, LF backing DC	1/8 to L (LF)	B	Q
6	Replace weight to RF	Facing against LOD	No turn	BF	Q

Notes

1 Steps 1-3 or 1-6 may be repeated

2 On 2 and 5 the turn of foot is reflected in the hips, the upper body remaining square to Man. The toe of back foot is opposite heel of front foot

3 It is important for Lady to respond to the Man's increased tone in arms with matching tone in her arms in order to accept the lead

4 If preferred the front foot may be drawn slightly towards back foot on 3 and 6

CLOSED ROCKS (continued)

Precedes (A)   Natural Basic Movement - 1-3 Reverse Basic Movement

       (L)   Argentine Crosses ended facing LOD, with LF Stationary Walk and Lady's underarm turn ending

       (F)   Natural Roll

Follows (A)   Natural Basic Movement - Corta Jaca (when near a corner)

       (L)   Open Rocks

       (F)   Natural Roll - Three Step Turn

Follows to 1-3

       (A&L)   Reverse Basic Movement - Reverse Turn

       (F)   Reverse Roll - Three Step Turn

17   OPEN ROCKS (L&F)

Commence in Closed Position. No Bounce

MAN	Foot Position	Alignment	Amount of Turn	Foot-work	Lead	Count
1	RF fwd	Facing LOD	No turn	BF	Increase tone in arms and exert pressure through L hand to turn Lady R, then release L to R hold	S
2	LF fwd, small step	"	"	BF	Support Lady with R arm	Q
3	Replace weight to RF, toe slightly turned out	Against LOD	"	B	Exert slight pressure through R hand to comm-ence to turn Lady L	Q

OPEN ROCKS (continued)

MAN	Foot Position	Alignment	Amount of Turn	Foot-work	Lead	Count
4	LF fwd	Facing LOD	"	BF	With R hand turn Lady L and place L hand on her back, then release hold with R hand	S
5	RF fwd, small step	"	"	BF	Support Lady with L arm	Q
6	Replace weight to LF, toe slightly turned out	Against LOD	No turn	B	Exert slight pressure through L hand to comm-ence to turn Lady R	Q

OPEN ROCKS (continued)

MAN	Foot Position	Alignment	Amount of Turn	Foot-work	Lead	Count
7	RF fwd	Facing LOD	"	BF	With L hand turn Lady R and place R hand on her back, then release hold with L hand	S
8	LF fwd, small step	"	"	BF	Support Lady with R arm	Q
9	Replace weight to RF, toe slightly turned out	Against LOD	"	B	Exert slight pressure through R hand to comm-ence to turn Lady L	Q

OPEN ROCKS (continued)

LADY	Foot Position	Alignment	Amount of Turn	Footwork	Count
1	LF back	Commence backing LOD and turn to back DW	1/8 to R	BF	S
2	RF back at a 90° angle to Man on his R side. Small step, toe turned out	To wall	1/8 to R between 1 & 2	B	Q
3	Replace weight to LF	Facing DC against LOD	Commence to turn L (See note 1)	BF	Q
4	RF back and slightly to side	Backing DC	1/4 to L between 3 & 4	BF	S
5	LF back at a 90° angle to Man on his L side. Small step, toe turned out	To centre	1/8 to L between 4 & 5	B	Q
6	Replace weight to RF	Facing DW against LOD	Commence to turn R (See note 1)	BF	Q

OPEN ROCKS (continued)

LADY	Foot Position	Alignment	Amount of Turn	Footwork	Count
7	LF back and slightly to side	Backing DW	1/4 to R between 6 & 7	BF	S
8	RF back at a 90° angle to Man on his R side. Small step, toe turned out	To wall	1/8 to R between 7 & 8	B	Q
9	Replace weight to LF	Facing DC against LOD	Commence to turn L	BF	Q

Notes

1   On 2 LF remains backing DW as RF and body continue to turn R, therefore the turn between 3 & 4 is measured from the alignment of the front foot
Likewise, on 5, RF remains backing DC

2   It is important for the Lady to respond to Man's increased tone in his arms with matching tone in her arms, in order to accept the lead on 1. On 4 she places R hand on Man's L shoulder, immediately releasing L hand contact. On 7 she places L hand on Man's R shoulder, immediately releasing R hand contact

3   Lady's knee straightens and her heel lowers towards the floor on 2, 5 & 8 (The heel may lightly touch the floor)

4   First step of following figure is back and slightly to side

OPEN ROCKS (contiued)

Precedes (L)   Natural Basic Movement - 1-3 Reverse Basic Movement - Closed Rocks - Argentine Crosses ended facing LOD, with LF Stationary Walk and Lady's underarm turn ending

(F)   Natural Roll

Follows (L)   Reverse Turn (Man 1/8 L, Lady 1/4) between preceding step and 1, regaining normal hold

(F)   Reverse Roll (turn as above) - Three Step Turn

Follows to 1-6

(F)   Natural Roll (Man 1/8 R, Lady 1/4) between preceding step & 1, regaining normal hold - Counter Promenade Runs, starting with 7-9 and continuing with 4-9

Commence in Closed Position. Use "Polka" Bounce

MAN	Foot Position	Alignment	Amount of Turn	Foot-work	Lead	Count
1	RF back	Commence backing DW and turn to back LOD	1/8 to L	BF	Weight change	S
2	Replace weight to LF, having moved it slightly leftwards	Facing DW against LOD	1/8 to L between 1 & 2	BF	"	Q
3	Replace weight to RF	Backing DC	No turn	BF	"	Q
4	LF back	Backing LOD	1/8 to R between 3 & 4	BF	"	S
5	Replace weight to RF, having moved it slightly rightwards	Facing DC against LOD	1/8 to R between 4 & 5	BF	"	Q
6	Replace weight to LF	Backing DW	No turn	BF	"	Q

1-3 or 1-6 may be repeated
Note
On 2 & 5 the Man slightly extends hold to allow Lady to place full weight on to her back foot
Polka Bounce
Each step is taken with strong pressure through ball of foot, lightly lowering heel on the second half of step

BACK ROCKS (continued)

LADY	Foot Position	Alignment	Amount of Turn	Footwork	Count
1	LF fwd	Commence facing DW and turn to face LOD	1/8 to L	BF	S
2	Replace weight to RF, having moved it slightly rightwards	Backing DW against LOD	1/8 to L between 1 & 2	BF	Q
3	Replace weight to LF	Facing DC	No turn	BF	Q
4	RF fwd	Facing LOD	1/8 to R between 3 & 4	BF	S
5	Replace weight to LF, having moved it slightly leftwards	Backing DC against LOD	1/8 to R between 4 & 5	BF	Q
6	Replace weight to RF	Facing DW	No turn	BF	Q

1-3 or 1-6 may be repeated

Polka Bounce

Each step is taken with strong pressure through ball of foot, lightly lowering heel on the second half of step

BACK ROCKS (continued)

Note Man and Lady

The pelvis swings naturally towards the stepping foot on 1 and 2 and commences to return to normal position on 3.   This action is repeated on 4-6 (The pelvic action is slight, not exaggerated)

Precedes (L)		1-3 Reverse Basic Movement - 1-3 Reverse Turn
	(F)	1-3 Reverse Roll
Follows (L)		4-6 Reverse Basic Movement - 4-6 Reverse Turn - Plait
	(F)	4-6 Reverse Roll

From step 3

	(L)	4-6 Natural Basic Movement
	(F)	4-6 Natural Roll

Back Rocks may commence with LF (Lady RF) from step 4

Precedes (L)	1-3 Natural Basic Movement
(F)	1-3 Natural Roll

NOTES

Commence in Closed Position. No Bounce action

MAN	Foot Position	Alignment	Amount of Turn	Foot-work	Lead	Count
1	RF back, small step, with part weight	Commence backing DW and turn to back LOD	1/8 to L	Press - ure on B of RF	Weight change, increas- ing tone and slightly extend- ing arms	S
2	Taking full weight to RF, LF back, small step, with part weight	Backing LOD	No turn	Lower R heel. Press - ure on B of LF	Weight change	S
3	Taking full weight to LF, RF back, small step, with part weight	"	"	Lower L heel. Press - ure on B of RF	"	Q
4.5	Repeat steps 2 & 3	"	"	Repeat 2 & 3	"	QS

May be repeated, commencing with LF

PLAIT (continued)

MAN

Merengue action is used on each step as follows

1   L knee is firmly straightened on second half of preceding step, causing L hip to move back and to L, then RF is placed back with knee flexed

2   R knee is firmly straightened on second half of preceding step, causing R hip to move back and to R, then LF is placed back with knee flexed

The natural reaction in Man's body to the straightening and flexing of knees indicates the turn for Lady

Notes

1   The first step is slightly longer to create space between Man and Lady

2   The Plait may commence with LF

3   Lower heel and take full weight on to foot when commencing first step of following figure

4   L to R hand hold may be used

PLAIT (continued)

LADY	Foot Position	Alignment	Amount of Turn	Footwork	Count
1	Swivel to L on RF and LF fwd, small step	Commence facing DW and turn to face DC	1/4 to L	B	S
2	Swivel to R on LF and RF fwd, small step, having brushed LF	Facing DW	1/4 to R	B	S
3	Swivel to L on RF and LF fwd, small step, having brushed RF	Facing DC	1/4 to L	B	Q
4-5	Repeat steps 2 & 3	As 2 & 3	As 2 & 3	As 2 & 3	QS

May be repeated, commencing with LF

Action used on each step as follows
1   Swivel on RF on second half of preceding step and LF fwd, knee straight
2   Swivel on LF on second half of preceding step and RF fwd, knee straight

Points to remember
The knee is slightly flexed as foot tracks under body passing other foot
Turn is initiated in the feet which are parallel throughout
There is no turn in upper body. Shoulders remain square to partner. Retain upright position

Note   When Plait is not repeated last step is BF
If preferred heels may lightly touch the floor on each step

PLAIT (contiued)

Precedes (when commenced with RF)

(L)	1-3 Reverse Basic Movement - 1-3 Reverse Turn - Back Rocks
(F)	1-3 Reverse Roll

Precedes (when commenced with LF)

(L)	1-3 Natural Basic Movement - 1-3 Back Rocks
(F)	1-3 Natural Roll

Follows (when ended with LF)

(L)	4-6 Reverse Basic Movement - 4-6 Reverse Turn
(F)	4-6 Reverse Roll

Follows(when ended with RF)

(L)	4-6 Natural Basic Movement
(F)	4-6 Natural Roll

Notes   Man and Lady

1   When repeated the Plait may be gradually curved 1/4 left around a corner

2   There is no turn on 1 when Plait is repeated

Commence in Right Side Position with Double hand hold, Man's R arm behind Lady's back at waist level, Lady's arms crossed in front of body. No Bounce

MAN	Foot Position	Alignment	Amount of Turn	Foot-work	Lead	Count
1-3	Whisk to L End in RSP	Facing LOD	No turn	See note 3 below	Release hold with L hand and extend R arm to R side at waist level	1.2.3
4-6	Whisk to R. End in RSP	"	"	See note 3 below	Return R arm to comm-encing position and take Double hand hold again	1.2.3

Note

Because of the timing the following differences occur on the Whisks

1   There is no Bounce action

2   Part weight is taken on to steps 2 & 5

3   The footwork on step 2 is ball of foot

ROLLING OFF THE ARM (continued)

LADY	Foot Position	Alignment	Amount of Turn	Footwork	Count
1	RF fwd	Commence facing LOD and turn to face wall	1/4 to R	BF, then turn on B of RF (foot flat)	1
2	Close LF to RF	Backing LOD	1/4 to R between 1 & 2	B	2
3	RF to side and close LF to RF without weight in RSP. L knee veers inwards	Facing LOD	1/2 to R between 2 & 3	BF (I/E of B, LF)	3
4	LF fwd	Facing centre	1/4 to L between 3 & 4	BF, then turn on B of LF (foot flat)	1
5	Close RF to LF	Backing LOD	1/4 to L between 4 & 5	B	2
6	LF to side and close RF to LF without weight in RSP. R knee veers inwards	Facing LOD	1/2 to L between 5 & 6	BF (I/E of B, RF)	3

ROLLING OFF THE ARM (continued)

Precedes (L&F)   Criss Cross Bota Fogos and LF Stationary Walk with Lady's underarm turn ending, finished in RSP, taking Double hand hold. Continue with a Samba Walk (or three Samba Walks) in RSP - Criss Cross Voltas ended in RSP with Double hand hold

Follow   (L&F)   Two Samba Walks in RSP commenced with LF (Lady RF) and then repeat Rolling off the Arm with one of the endings described below Alternatively dance Rolling off the Arm once only, using one of the endings below

Ending 1 Closed Position to follow with a Whisk to L

Man turn 1/4 R over 4-6 to face wall, continuing to turn Lady L on 6, releasing R to L hand hold and keeping R hand lightly in contact with Lady as she turns within the circle of R arm. Regain normal hold in Closed Position at the end of Lady's turn. (Lady continue to turn an extra 1/4 L on LF on 6 to end facing centre with LF in front of RF in Cuban Cross position)

Ending 2 Closed Position to follow with a Reverse Turn

Man lead Lady to turn L and to move well
fwd DC on 4, then continue to turn Lady
strongly to L over 5 and 6, releasing R to L
hand hold, keeping R hand lightly in contact
with Lady as she turns within the circle of R
arm. Regain normal hold in Closed Position
at the end of Lady's turn.

Lady 4 LF fwd (1/8 L to face DC)

5 RF side having turned 3/8 L to back LOD

6 LF side in front of Man, having turned 1/2
L to face LOD, then continue to turn an extra
1/2 L on LF to end facing against LOD with
LF in front of RF in Cuban Cross position

(L) Ending 3   **Right Shadow Position**

Having danced Foot Change 8 (see page 76)

Commence in Closed Position. No Bounce

MAN	Foot Position	Alignment	Amount of Turn	Foot-work	Lead	Count
1	LF fwd, toe turned out	To wall	Commence to turn to R on 1	BF	Slight press-ure with R hand to lead Lady fwd	Q
2	RF behind LF (Cuban Cross)	Facing DW against LOD	1/8 to R between 1 & 2	B	Weight change	Q
3	LF to side and slightly fwd	Facing against LOD	1/8 to R between 2 & 3	BF	"	S
4	RF fwd in line with LF, small step. Toe turned out	To centre	1/4 to R between 3 & 4	BF	Slight press-ure with R hand to lead Lady fwd	Q
5	LF to side and slightly back	Facing DC	1/8 to R between 4 & 5	B	Weight change	Q
6	RF fwd in line with LF, small step. Toe turned out	Down LOD	1/8 to R between 5 & 6	BF	"	S

MAN	Foot Position	Alignment	Amount of Turn	Foot-work	Lead	Count
7	LF fwd, toe turned out	Down LOD	Continue to turn to R on 7	BF	Slight pressure with R hand to lead Lady fwd	Q
8	RF behind LF (Cuban Cross)	Facing DW	1/8 to R between 7 & 8	B	Weight change	Q
9	LF to side and slightly fwd	Facing wall	1/8 to R between 8 & 9	BF	"	S
10	RF fwd in line with LF, small step. Toe turned out	Against LOD	1/4 to R between 9 & 10	BF	Slight pressure with R hand to lead Lady fwd	Q
11	LF to side and slightly back	Facing DC against LOD	1/8 to R between 10 & 11	B	Weight change	Q
12	RF fwd in line with LF, small step. Toe turned out	Facing centre	1/8 to R between 11 & 12	BF	"	S

Notes

1 Incline body slightly L over 1-3 and 7-9, and R over 4 -6 and 10-12

2 More turn could be made (up to two complete turns over 1-12) and other alignments may be used

ARGENTINE CROSSES (continued)

LADY	Foot Position	Alignment	Amount of Turn	Footwork	Count
1	RF fwd in line with LF, small step. Toe turned out	To centre	Commence to turn to R on 1	BF	Q
2	LF to side and slightly back	Facing DC	1/8 to R between 1 & 2	B	Q
3	RF fwd in line with LF, small step. Toe turned out	Down LOD	1/8 to R between 2 & 3	BF	S
4	LF fwd, toe turned out	To wall	1/4 to R between 3 & 4	BF	Q
5	RF behind LF (Cuban Cross)	Facing DW against LOD	1/8 to R between 4 & 5	B	Q
6	LF to side and slightly fwd	Facing against LOD	1/8 to R between 5 & 6	BF	S

ARGENTINE CROSSES (continued)

LADY	Foot Position	Alignment	Amount of Turn	Footwork	Count
7	RF fwd in line with LF, small step. Toe turned out	Against LOD	Continue to turn to R on 7	BF	Q
8	LF to side and slightly back	Facing DC against LOD	1/8 to R between 7 & 8	B	Q
9	RF fwd in line with LF, small step. Toe turned out	To centre	1/8 to R between 8 & 9	BF	S
10	LF fwd, toe turned out	Down LOD	1/4 to R between 9 & 10	BF	Q
11	RF behind LF (Cuban Cross)	Facing DW	1/8 to R between 10 & 11	B	Q
12	LF to side and slightly fwd	Facing wall	1/8 to R between 11 & 12	BF	S

Note

1 Incline body slightly R over 1-3 and 7-9, and L over 4-6 and 10-12

2 More turn could be made (up to two complete turns over 1-12) and other alignments may be used

ARGENTINE CROSSES (continued)

Precedes (L&F)   Whisk to R - Side Samba Walk (Man 1/4 R
                       Lady 1/4 L) - RF Stationary Samba Walk -
                       Criss Cross Voltas - Solo Spot Volta to R
                       (Lady L)

Follows   (L&F)   Whisk to L (with or without Lady's under -
                       arm turn)- LF Stationary Samba Walk
                       leading Lady underarm into Spot Volta to R,
                       releasing hold with R hand.   Regain normal
                       hold in Closed Position and follow with any
                       syllabus figure commenced with RF, depend-
                       ing on finishing alignment of Argentine
                       Crosses

Follows to 1-9

(L&F)   Whisk to R (with or without Lady's under -
                       arm turn) - RF Stationary Samba Walk
                       leading Lady underarm into Spot Volta to L,
                       releasing hold with R hand

**The Argentine Crosses may be commenced with RF (Lady
LF) dancing steps 4-12**

Precedes (L&F)   Whisk to L - LF Stationary Walk - Solo Spot
                       Volta to L (Lady to R)

Development (F)

Over 4-6 Man may turn Lady to L under raised L arm, releasing
hold with R hand (Lady LF fwd into a Bota Fogo turning 1/2 to L to
end facing Man again). Regain normal hold and continue with 7-12
(or repeat Lady's underarm turn again over 10-12)

NOTES

MAYPOLE (MAN TURNING LEFT)

Commence in Open PP, L to R hand hold. Use Bounce action

Man dances a Circular Volta commenced with LF and turned to L,circling around Lady while leading her to dance a Spot Volta turning R under raised arms

End in Closed Position regaining normal hold

The Maypole may be danced over two, three or four bars of music, therefore finishing alignments and amounts of turn are flexible. Teaching counts as follows

"1 a 2 a 3 a 4" (2 bars)   "1 a 2 a 3 a 4 a 5 a 6" (3 bars)
"1 a 2 a 3 a 4 a 5 a 6 a 7 a 8" (4 bars)

Precedes (L&F)	Side Samba Walk - Criss Cross Bota Fogos - Criss Cross Voltas ended in Open PP (The Maypole may also commence facing partner following a RF Stationary Samba Walk)
Follows (L&F)	Any syllabus figure commenced with RF when facing partner, depending on alignment

MAYPOLE (continued)

MAYPOLE (MAN TURNING RIGHT)

Commence in Open CPP, L to R hand hold. Use Bounce action

Man dances a Circular Volta commenced with RF and turned to R, circling around Lady while leading her to dance a Spot Volta turning L under raised arms

End in Closed Position regaining normal hold

The Maypole may be danced over two, three or four bars of music, therefore finishing alignments and amounts of turn are flexible. Teaching counts as follows

"1 a 2 a 3 a 4" (2 bars)   " 1 a 2 a 3 a 4 a 5 a 6" (3 bars)
"1 a 2 a 3 a 4 a 5 a 6 a 7 a 8" (4 bars)

Precedes (L)	Criss Cross Bota Fogos or Criss Cross Voltas ended in Open CPP (The Maypole may also commence facing partner following a LF Stationary Samba Walk)
(F)	Samba Locks
Follows (L&F)	Any syllabus figure commenced with LF when facing partner, depending on alignment

This is a Circular Volta danced in R Shadow Position, Man and Lady using the same foot. It may commence with RF, moving to left, circling up to a complete turn to R over 1-7, or commenced with LF, moving to right, circling up to a complete turn to L

The Circular Volta may be continued for one or two additional bars of music

Precedes to Circular Volta commenced with RF

(A)	Foot Change 1 (Closed Position to R Shadow Position)
(L&F)	Foot Change 8 (RSP to R Shadow Position)

Precedes when already in R Shadow Position, using same foot as partner

(A)	LF Samba Walk - LF Travelling Bota Fogo Fwd - Shadow Travelling Volta commenced with LF
(L)	Shadow Circular Volta commenced with LF
(F)	Cruzado Walks or Locks ended with weight on LF

Follows (all on same foot as partner)

(A)	LF Samba Walk - LF Travelling Bota Fogo Fwd - Shadow Travelling Volta commenced with LF
(L)	Shadow Circular Volta commenced with LF
(F)	"Same Foot" Bota Fogo to R Contra Position - Cruzado Walks or Locks commenced with LF

SHADOW CIRCULAR VOLTA (L&F)

Precedes to Circular Volta commenced with LF

(L&F)	Foot Change 3 (PP or Open PP to R Shadow Position)

Precedes when already in R Shadow Position(all on same foot as partner)

(L)	RF Samba Walk - RF Travelling Bota Fogo Fwd - Shadow Travelling or Circular Volta commenced with RF
(F)	Cruzado Walks or Locks ended with weight on RF

Follows

(L&F)	Foot Change 2 (R Shadow Position to Closed Position) - Foot Change 4 (R Shadow Position to PP)

Follows (all on same foot as partner)

(L)	RF Samba Walk - RF Travelling Bota Fogo Fwd - Shadow Travelling or Circular Volta commenced with RF
(F)	"Same Foot" Bota Fogo to R Contra Position - Cruzado Walks or Locks commenced with RF

Note

The last two steps of Shadow Circular Volta may be replaced with 2 & 3 of a Bota Fogo. Amount of Turn remains unchanged

Commence in R Contra Position. Use Bounce action

MAN	Foot Position	Alignment	Amount of Turn	Foot-work	Lead	Count
1	RF fwd towards Lady's R side in R Contra Position	Facing DW	No turn	BF	Slight press-ure with R hand to lead Lady fwd	1
2	LF back and slightly to side without weight. Toe turned out	Towards alignment of 3	1/4 to R over 2 & 3	I/E of T (Press-ure)	Slightly extend hold over 2 & 3	a
3	Take minimal weight to LF and replace weight to RF in L Contra Position, having moved it slightly back	Facing DW against LOD		BF		2

CONTRA BOTA FOGOS (continued)

MAN	Foot Position	Alignment	Amount of Turn	Foot-work	Lead	Count
4	LF fwd towards Lady's L side in L Contra Position	"	No turn	BF	Slight press-ure with R hand to lead Lady fwd, return-ing arms to normal position	1
5	RF back and slightly to side without weight. Toe turned out	Towards alignment of 6	1/4 to L over 5 & 6	I/E of T (Press-ure)	Slightly extend hold over 5 & 6	a
6	Take minimal weight to RF and replace weight to LF in R Contra Position, having moved it slightly back	Facing DW		BF		2

1-3 or 1-6 may be repeated

120

CONTRA BOTA FOGOS (continued)

LADY	Foot Position	Alignment	Amount of Turn	Footwork	Count
1	RF fwd towards Man's R side in R Contra Position	Facing DC against LOD	No turn	BF	1
2	LF back and slightly to side without weight. Toe turned out	Towards alignment of 3	1/4 to R over 2 & 3	I/E of T (Pressure)	a
3	Take minimal weight to LF and replace weight to RF in L Contra Position, having moved it slightly back	Facing DC		BF	2
4	LF fwd towards Man's L side in L Contra Position	"	No turn	BF	1
5	RF back and slightly to side without weight. Toe turned out	Towards alignment of 6	1/4 to L over 5 & 6	I/E of T (Pressure)	a
6	Take minimal weight to RF and replace weight to LF in R Contra Position, having moved it slightly back	Facing DC against LOD		BF	2

1-3 or 1-6 may be repeated

CONTRA BOTA FOGOS (continued)

Precedes (F)		Foot Change 5 (from PP to R Contra Position) - Roundabout to L - "Same Foot" LF Bota Fogo from R Shadow Position to R Contra Position
Follows	**(F)**	Foot Change 6 (from R Contra Position to PP) - Foot Change 7 (from R Contra Position to Open CPP) - Roundabout to R

Follows to 1-3 (RF Contra Bota Fogo)

(F)   Roundabout to L

Precedes to 4-6 (LF Contra Bota Fogo)

(F)   Roundabout to R - "Same Foot" RF Bota Fogo from R Shadow Position to L Contra Position

Development

Contra Bota Fogos may be danced with hand changes as follows:-

Commence with R to R hand hold achieving this at the end of the preceding figure
Change to L to L hand hold on 3
Change to R to R hand hold on 6

When danced in this manner the Contra Bota Fogos are usually repeated, regaining normal hold on last step

ROUNDABOUT TO RIGHT

Commence in R Contra Position. Use Bounce action

MAN	Foot Position	Alignment	Amount of Turn	Foot-work	Lead	Count
1-5	1-5 of Circular Volta in R Contra Position, commenced with RF	Commence facing DW. End facing LOD	7/8 to R over 1-5	As Volta Move-ment	Weight changes	1 a 2 a 1
6	LF to side without weight	Pointing DW. Body facing wall	3/8 to R over 6 & 7	I/E of T (Press-ure)	Move arms very slightly to R	a
7	Take minimal weight to LF and replace weight to RF in L Contra Position	Facing DW against LOD		BF	Weight change	2

LADY	Foot Position	Alignment	Amount of Turn	Footwork	Count
1-5	1-5 of Circular Volta in R Contra Position, commenced with RF	Commence facing DC against LOD. End facing against LOD	7/8 to R over 1-5	As Volta Movement	1 a 2 a 1
6	LF to side without weight	Pointing DC against LOD. Body facing centre	3/8 to R over 6 & 7	I/E of T (Pressure)	a
7	Take minimal weight to LF and replace weight to RF in L Contra Position	Facing DC		BF	2

Precedes (F)   Foot Change 5 (from PP to R Contra Position) - LF Contra Bota Fogo - Roundabout to L - "Same Foot" LF Bota Fogo from R Shadow Position to R Contra Position

Follows (F)   LF Contra Bota Fogo - Roundabout to L

Notes   **Man and Lady**

1   The teaching count of " 1 a 2 a 3 a 4" may be used

2   The Roundabout may be continued for two extra bars of music dancing 13 steps of Circular Volta before dancing the steps as described for 6 & 7. (Teaching count "1 a 2 a 3 a 4 a 5 a 6 a 7 a 8")

3   The couple circle around an imaginary spot between them, keeping the shoulders parallel

ROUNDABOUT TO LEFT (F)

Commence in L Contra Position. Use Bounce action

MAN	Foot Position	Alignment	Amount of Turn	Foot-work	Lead	Count
1-5	1-5 Circular Volta in L Contra Position, commenced with LF	Commence facing DW against LOD. End facing against LOD	7/8 to L over 1-5	As Volta Move-ment	Weight changes	1 a 2 a 1
6	RF to side without weight	Pointing DW against LOD. Body facing wall	3/8 to L over 6 & 7	I/E of T (Press-ure	Move arms very slightly to L	a
7	Take minimal weight to RF and replace weight to LF in R Contra Position	Facing DW		BF	Weight change	2

ROUNDABOUT TO LEFT(continued)

LADY	Foot Position	Alignment	Amount of Turn	Footwork	Count
1-5	1-5 Circular Volta in L Contra Position, commenced with LF	Commence facing DC. End facing LOD	7/8 to L over 1-5	As Volta Movement	1 a 2 a 1
6	RF to side without weight	Pointing DC. Body facing centre	3/8 to L over 6 & 7	I/E of T (Pressure)	a
7	Take minimal weight to RF and replace weight to LF in R Contra Position	Facing DC against LOD		BF	2

Precedes (F)   RF Contra Bota Fogo - Roundabout to R - "Same Foot" RF Bota Fogo from R Shadow Position to L Contra Position

Follows (F)   RF Contra Bota Fogo - Roundabout to R

Notes   **Man and Lady**

1   The teaching count of " 1 a 2 a 3 a 4" may be used

2   The Roundabout may be continued for two additional bars of music, dancing 13 steps of Circular Volta before dancing the steps as described for 6 & 7. (Teaching count "1 a 2 a 3 a 4 a 5 a 6 a 7 a 8")

3   The couple circle around an imaginary spot between them, keeping the shoulders parallel

Commence in Contact Position. No Bounce

MAN	Foot Position	Alignment	Amount of Turn	Foot-work	Lead	Count
1	RF fwd, leaning slightly back	Commence facing LOD and turn to face DW	1/8 to R	HF	Weight change	S
2	LF to side, leaning slightly R	Backing DC	1/4 to R between 1 & 2	BF	"	Q
3	Close RF to LF, preparing to lean fwd	Backing LOD	1/8 to R between 2 & 3	BF	"	Q
4	LF back, leaning slightly fwd	Backing DW	1/8 to R between 3 & 4	BF	"	S
5	RF to side, leaning slightly L	Pointing LOD	3/8 to R between 4 & 5. Body turns less	BF	"	Q
6	Close LF to RF, preparing to lean back	Facing LOD	Body completes turn	BF	"	Q

May be repeated

Notes

1 Knees are slightly more flexed during 1-3 and straighter during 4-6

2 There is a slight foot swivel on LF between 2 & 3

NATURAL ROLL (continued)

LADY	Foot Position	Alignment	Amount of Turn	Footwork	Count
1	LF back, leaning slightly fwd	Commence backing LOD and turn to back DW	1/8 to R	BF	S
2	RF to side, leaning slightly L	Pointing LOD	3/8 to R between 1 & 2. Body turns less	BF	Q
3	Close LF to RF, preparing to lean back	Facing LOD	Body completes turn	BF	Q
4	RF fwd, leaning slightly back	Facing DW	1/8 to R between 3 & 4	HF	S
5	LF to side, leaning slightly R	Backing DC	1/4 to R between 4 & 5	BF	Q
6	Close RF to LF, preparing to lean fwd	Backing LOD	1/8 to R between 5 & 6	BF	Q

May be repeated

Notes

1   Knees are straighter during 1-3 and slightly more flexed during 4-6

2   There is a slight foot swivel on LF between 5 & 6

NATURAL ROLL (continued)

Precedes (F)   Any syllabus figure ended facing partner
with weight on LF - 1-6 Open Rocks (Lady
turn 3/8 to R between preceding step and 1,
which will be back and slightly to side)

Precedes to 4-6

    (F)   Corta Jaca - 1-5 Plait - 1-3 Back Rocks

Follows   (F)   Any syllabus figure commenced with RF
when facing partner, depending on align-
ment

Follows to 1-3

    (F)   Back Rocks or Plait commenced with LF

Notes   Man and Lady

1   The Natural Roll may commence and finish
in other alignments, depending on the Precede or Follow used

2   Less turn may be made (minimum 1/2 over
1-6)

3   Due to the use of Contact Position arms are
held a little higher than normal

NOTES

Commence in Contact Position. No Bounce

The Foot Positions and other technical details of the Reverse Roll
are as for Reverse Turn, when the SQQSQQ timing is used

The characteristic roll of the body is created from the waist and is
as follows

MAN		**Count**
	Prepare for roll by inclining body R on last 1/4 beat of preceding step	
1	Fwd	S
2	Fwd and to L	Q
3	To L	Q
4	Back and to L	S
5	Back	Q
6	Back and to R	Q

LADY		
	Prepare for roll by inclining body L on last 1/4 beat of preceding step	
1	Back	S
2	Back and to R	Q
3	To R	Q
4	Fwd and to R	S
5	Fwd	Q
6	Fwd and to L	Q

Note   Man and Lady

The body inclination on 1 is fast and the L arm (Lady R arm) is
lowered, returning to normal position over 2 and 3 and raised again
over 4 and 5

(F)   Precedes and Follows as for Reverse Turn (page 80)

NOTES

Commence in Closed Position. No Bounce

MAN	Foot Position	Alignment	Amount of Turn	Foot-work	Lead	Count
1	RF to side	Facing wall	No turn	B	Weight change	1
2	Replace weight to LF in PP	Facing DW	1/8 to L between 1 & 2	BF	Weight change achieving PP, widening hold	2
3	RF fwd in Open PP and CBMP	Facing DW	Commence to turn R	BF	Achieve Open PP releasing L to R hand hold Extend L arm to side	3
4	LF back and slightly to side	Backing LOD	3/8 to R between 3 & 4	B	Achieve Closed Position and place L hand on Lady's R shoulder blade	1

PROMENADE AND COUNTER PROMENADE RUNS
(continued)

MAN	Foot Position	Alignment	Amount of Turn	Foot-work	Lead	Count
5	RF to side in Open CPP	Moving along LOD, facing DC	3/8 to R between 4 & 5	BF	Release contact with R hand and achieve Open CPP	2
6	LF fwd and and across in Open CPP and CBMP	Pointing LOD	1/8 to R between 5 & 6. Body turns less	BF	Maintain Open PP and extend R arm to side	3
7	RF fwd between partners feet	Facing LOD	Body completes turn	B	Achieve Closed Position and place R hand on Lady's L shoulder blade	1

PROMENADE AND COUNTER PROMENADE RUNS
(continued)

MAN	Foot Position	Alignment	Amount of Turn	Foot-work	Lead	Count
8	LF to side in Open PP	Moving along LOD, facing DW	1/8 to R between 7 & 8	BF	Achieve Open PP	2
9	RF fwd and across in Open PP and CBMP	"	No turn	BF	Maintain Open PP and extend L arm to side	3

Inclination of body

1.2	Normal position
3	Incline body to L
4	Maintain inclination to L
5	Return body to normal position
6	Incline body to R
7	Maintain inclination to R
8	Return body to normal position
9	Incline body to L

This shape could be reversed, inclining body to R on 3, to L on 6, and to R on 9

LADY	Foot Position	Alignment	Amount of Turn	Footwork	Count
1	LF to side	Facing centre	No turn	B	1
2	Replace weight to RF in PP	Facing DC	1/8 to R between 1 & 2	BF	2
3	LF fwd and across in Open PP and CBMP	Pointing LOD	1/8 to R between 2 & 3. Body turns less	BF	3
4	RF fwd between partner's feet	Facing LOD	Body completes turn	B	1
5	LF to side in Open CPP	Moving along LOD, facing DW	1/8 to R between 4 & 5	BF	2
6	RF fwd in Open PP and CBMP	Facing DW	Commence to turn R	BF	3
7	LF back and slightly to side	Backing LOD	3/8 to R between 6 & 7	B	1
8	RF to side in Open PP	Moving along LOD, facing DC	3/8 to R between 7 & 8	BF	2
9	LF fwd and across in Open PP and CBMP	"	No turn	BF	3

Inclination of body

1.2	Normal position
3	Incline body to R
4	Maintain inclination to R
5	Return body to normal position
6	Incline body to L
7	Maintain inclination to L
8	Return body to normal position
9	Incline body to R

This shape could be reversed, inclining body to L on 3, to R on 6, and to L on 9

Notes

1   Place right hand lightly on Man's left shoulder on 4, and place left hand lightly on Man's right shoulder on 7

2   Extend free arm to side to match Man's arm position on steps 3, 6, and 9

Precedes (F)   Natural Basic Movement - 1-3 Reverse Basic Movement - Whisk to L - Solo Spot Volta to L (Lady R) - Natural Roll

Follows (F)   Samba Walk in PP - Three Step Turn- turn to R (Lady L) to face partner to follow with Whisk to L - LF Rhythm Bounce - Volta travelling to L (Lady R) commencing with step 2

Note   Man and Lady
Man may step fwd (Lady back) on first step, taking second step to side in PP

NOTES

29   THREE STEP TURN (F)

This figure is used as an entry to the Samba Locks and is preceded by 1-3 of Closed or Open Rocks or Promenade and Counter Promenade Runs

Man dances a LF Stationary Walk (count "1 a 2") turning to left to face DC. During her turn Lady moves to Man's left side, to end in Open CPP

Lead
Turn Lady to L taking L to R hand hold, then release hold with R hand continuing to turn her strongly to L under raised L arm during step 1. Continue to turn Lady strongly to L on 2 & 3, lowering L arm at the end of her turn
(Note when preceded by the Closed Rock Man is already holding Lady's R hand in his L hand)

LADY'S STEPS (No Bounce)	**Count**
1 RF to side turning L to face against LOD, then continue to turn 5/8 L on RF to face DC (Spiral action)	1
2 LF fwd continuing to turn L to face centre	2
3 RF to side turning 1/4 L to face against LOD, then continue to turn 3/8 L on RF to face DW (Spiral action)	3

Footwork
1   BF, then turn on B of RF with foot flat (T of LF)

2   BF

3   BF, then turn on B of RF with foot flat (T of LF)

Note difference in timing for Man and Lady

NOTES

Commence in Open Counter Promenade Position. No Bounce

MAN	Foot Position	Alignment	Amount of Turn	Foot-work	Lead	Count
1	RF fwd, part weight. Toe turned out	Commence facing DC. Down LOD, body facing DW	1/8 to R on LF. Body and RF turn more	BF	Extend joined arms fwd down LOD, below shoulder level	Q
2	LF behind RF (Cuban Cross)	Down LOD, body facing DW	No turn	T	Weight change, retaining arm position	Q
3	RF fwd, small step. Toe turned out	"	"	BF	"	S
4	LF fwd, part weight, in Open CPP. Toe turned out	Down LOD, body facing DC	1/8 to L on RF. Body and LF turn more	BF	Extend joined arms back against LOD	Q
5	RF behind LF in Open CPP (Cuban Cross)	"	No turn	T	Weight change, retaining arm position	Q
6	LF fwd, small step, in Open CPP. Toe turned out	"	"	BF	"	S
7-12	As 1-6. End in Open CPP	As 1-6	As 1-6	As 1-6	As 1-6	QQS QQS

SAMBA LOCKS (continued)

LADY	Foot Position	Alignment	Amount of Turn	Footwork	Count
1	LF fwd, part weight. Toe turned out	Commence facing DW. Down LOD, body facing DC	1/8 to L on RF. Body and LF turn more	BF	Q
2	RF behind LF (Cuban Cross)	Down LOD, body facing DC	No turn	T	Q
3	LF fwd, small step. Toe turned out	"	"	BF	S
4	RF fwd, part weight in Open CPP. Toe turned out	Down LOD, body facing DW	1/8 to R on LF. Body and RF turn more	BF	Q
5	LF behind RF in Open CPP (Cuban Cross)	"	No turn	T	Q
6	RF fwd, small step in Open CPP. Toe turned out	"	"	BF	S
7-12	As 1-6. End in Open CPP	As 1-6	As 1-6	As 1-6	QQS QQS

Note   Man and Lady
The free arm is extended to side, just below shoulder level, to
match partner's arm line

SAMBA LOCKS (continued)

Precedes   **(F)**   1-3 Criss Cross Bota Fogos - 1-7 Criss Cross Voltas - Three Step Turn

Follows   **(F)**   Criss Cross Bota Fogos started from step 4 - Criss Cross Voltas started from step 8 - Maypole (Man turning R) Solo Spot Volta R (Lady L)

Note   **Man and Lady**

Turn on 1,4,7 and 12 is made towards end of previous beat of music and refers to the back foot. The turn out of front foot does not constitute an amount of turn

NOTES

The above figures are danced in Right Shadow Position, Man and Lady using the same foot

Cruzados Walks are two steps forward commenced with either foot and counted " S . S". They may be repeated

The action used is known as the "Cruzados action" and is described here in detail

Commence, for example, facing LOD, weight on LF with knee flexed. RF extended back with toe and leg turned out and pressure on inside edge of toe

		Rhythmic action count
1	Using pressure through ball of LF release L heel and commence to straighten knees, moving RF fwd on toe until it is level with LF, at the same time moving pelvis slightly fwd. (At this point body, hips, knees and toes are facing LOD)	a
2	Continue to straighten knees moving RF fwd on ball of foot, arriving at the 'top' of the bounce with R heel lightly in contact with floor. Weight central, both legs straight but not braced	S
3	Transfer weight fwd to RF flexing knee, arriving at the lowest point of the bounce. Allow the back foot and leg to turn out, completing a rotational hip movement. Return pelvis to normal position. Retain tone in back leg with pressure on inside edge of toe Repeat with LF	and

Two or four Cruzados Walks may precede or follow Cruzados Locks

Cruzados Locks

The foot positions and timing are as for Samba Locks although the front toe is not turned out. There is no turn and they may commence with either foot

The Cruzados action on the Locks is described in detail on next page (Note points 1,2 & 5 are as points 1,2 & 3 described for Cruzados Walks)

Cruzados Locks action

Commence as for Cruzados Walks

		Rhythmic action count
1	Using pressure through ball of LF release L heel and commence to straighten knees, moving RF fwd on toe until it is level with LF, at the same time moving pelvis slightly fwd. (At this point body, hips,knees and toes are facing LOD)	a
2	Continue to straighten knees moving RF fwd on ball of foot, arriving at the 'top' of the bounce with R heel lightly in contact with floor. Weight central, both legs straight but not braced	Q
3	Transfer weight fwd to RF flexing knee, at the same time placing LF behind RF (Cuban Cross) arriving at lowest point of the bounce	Q
4	Using pressure through ball of LF commence to straighten knees and move RF slightly fwd on ball of foot, arriving at the 'top' of the bounce with R heel lightly in contact with floor. Weight central, both legs straight but not braced	S
5	Transfer weight fwd to RF flexing knee, arriving at the lowest point of the bounce. Allow the back foot and leg to turn out, completing a rotational hip movement. Return pelvis to normal position. Retain tone in back leg with pressure on inside edge of toe Repeat commencing with LF	and

CRUZADOS WALKS AND LOCKS (continued)

Precedes and Follows (F)

Cruzados Walks and Locks are normally danced facing LOD from a
Foot Change to R Shadow Position (no 1 or 8) or any figure that
may be danced in R Shadow Position as listed
Follow with a Foot Change (no 2 or 4) or any figure that may be
danced in R Shadow Position using same foot as partner

Note   Hold may be released, adjusting to Right Side Position